"I'm so thankful that [...] widespread but rarely [...] women (yes—even Christian women!) today. Her biblical insight, honest personal testimony and extremely wise, practical advice are for you, whether you are in the throes of a porn addiction, engaging in an occasional fantasy world, one click away from investigating what all the fuss is about, or eager to help other women in the battle for purity. My prayer is that God would use this book to encourage us to pursue purity at levels often neglected in our discipleship."
Hilary Nicholls, founder of FrockChicks

"This is a book that addresses issues that women are grappling with—and all too often on their own. The church needs to wake up to the reality that pornography is not just a man's problem and that the popularity of women's erotica is reaching epidemic proportions in our culture. Written with an understanding of the issues involved, Helen is convinced that the gospel of Christ provides the only way out for people caught up in a life of sexual fantasy—and offers something much more intoxicating."
Carrie Sandom, Director of Women's Ministry, Cornhill Training Course, London

"At last, a book on sexual temptation for women (though there's much for men to learn here as well). *Purity Is Possible* is honest, real, realistic—all of which makes the hope that it offers truly hopeful. Above all, it points to the freedom and purity that we find through faith in the work of Jesus."
Tim Chester, author of *Captured by a Better Vision: Living Porn Free* and *Enjoying God*

"Helen rivets biblical truth to life with courage and conviction, warmth and humility. Exposing the destructive nature of female sexual fantasy as a disorder of worship often fuelled by pornography, she shows what it looks like for us to live out the gospel of Christ in sexual purity. Warmly recommended."
Sally Orwin Lee, Biblical Counselling UK

"This is a great book; realistic, honest, wise, warm and joyful. If this area is one you're struggling in, I hope you feel able to pick it up and read it—Helen understands where you're at, and how you're feeling, and can point you to real help and hope."
Andrea Trevenna, Associate Ministry for Women at St Nicholas Church, Sevenoaks, Kent; author of *The Heart of Singleness*

"We have many reasons to be grateful to Helen for this book. She writes with personal honesty, which will get us talking about a virtually ignored struggle. She writes wisely and perceptively, which means those conversations will be pastorally rich and biblically faithful. And she writes practically about the gospel of grace, which means women will be helped to change. Buy it and use it, not simply to escape the snare of sexual fantasy, but to find something better."
Steve Midgley, Minister of Christ Church, Cambridge

PURITY

IS POSSIBLE

HELEN THORNE

Purity is possible: *How to live free of the fantasy trap*
© Helen Thorne, 2014. Reprinted 2019 (twice).

Published by:
The Good Book Company

thegoodbook.com | www.thegoodbook.co.uk
thegoodbook.com.au | thegoodbook.co.nz | thegoodbook.co.in

ISBN: 9781909919846 | Printed in the UK

Cover design by ninefootone creative.
Design and art direction by André Parker

Contents

Introduction

There is a rumour going round that women don't watch online sex. There's a school of thought that says that our fantasies are romantic rather than explicit. Some argue that we don't think as visually as men, so pornography is rarely appealing. A few believe that we are, by nature, more pure and innocent.

I wish the rumours were right. They're not. Not in my experience, and not in the experience of most women I know.

I'm going to be honest with you because in what follows, I'm going to be asking you to be honest with yourself. In the past:

1. I have created sexual fantasies in my mind.
2. I have read women's erotica.
3. I have watched porn on the web.

And I've enjoyed it.

I know I'm not alone. An increasing number of women are watching internet pornography. One in three visitors to porn sites are female, according to a 2007 Nielson study. Gone are the days when films were just made by men for men. There are now alternatives to the seedy scenarios where blondes swoon at the first glimpse of the photocopier repair-man and give in to his every whim. Now female directors are producing short pieces that are specifically designed to arouse pleasure in women. The material is sensitive, sensual… appealing.

And many Christian women are no strangers to these sites. A survey in 2006 conducted by ChristiaNet found that 20% of Christian women use pornography regularly, and other surveys have produced a similar figure. That is one in five of us—perhaps it's you. My own experience in women's ministry would suggest that the true figure is much higher.

Even more of us are reading erotica. We tend not to call it that—it sounds better to refer to it as "romance", or simply as the latest bestseller—but reading it we are. *Fifty Shades of Grey* became the bestselling book in both Britain and the USA in 2012, and women consumed it avidly at home, on the bus and during lunchtimes at work. A book soaked through with explicit scenes, including violent sexual encounters, became the must-have novel of the year. And with *Fifty Shades of Grey*, explicit erotica became socially acceptable. Society attached no shame to reading and enjoying it—and millions did. Maybe you were one of them.

But maybe you weren't. Perhaps you've never visited a porn site, and never read an erotic novel, and never even wanted to. You picked up this book because it mentioned "fantasy" on the front (and now you're wondering whether this book is for you). Yet there are many, many more women who don't watch or read porn, but who write it—not on paper for publication, but in our minds for private enjoyment. It's sexual fantasy.

By sexual fantasy, I don't mean remembering a past sexual experience with a smile, or looking forward to sex with anticipation. I mean constructing a fantasy world—a better sex life—than our reality. I mean when we daydream about a different us, having a different sex life to the one that exists in the real world. That's sexual fantasising. For some, it's a fleeting thought; for others, a complex web of characters and intrigue that preoccupies our waking hours and leaves us feeling simultaneously intoxicated and disgusted.

The trouble is, few of us admit to any of this. Few of us feel we *can* admit to it, because no one ever talks about it. Churches certainly don't. When it comes to men, there's an acceptance that porn use is a common struggle. It's OK to admit to it, to talk about it, to get help with it.

Not for us. Women's struggles in this area are hardly ever mentioned, preached about, or made the focus of a conference. It's the great unspoken issue of our technological age.

So I want to say thank you for picking this book up and starting to read it. If you are using porn, reading erotica, or constructing sexual fantasies—whether you feel trapped in it, or whether you're not even sure it's that bad—you are in the same position as thousands and thousands of other women. You'll read about some of them in this book (all of their names have been changed, but they are all real women). You are not alone. And you have been pretty courageous just by getting a copy of this book, and opening up the first page. Thank you.

I don't think reading this book will be easy for you. It wasn't easy for me to write, because it brought me face to face with who I am. But it will take you on an exciting journey into freedom. You can leave excuses behind, and you can leave guilt behind. You can start walking with me towards a place far more intoxicating than pornography—a place that is full of love, free from guilt and grounded in utter security.

You can discover that, for all of us, and no matter what you've done, a beautiful purity *is* possible.

1. Beauty

We were designed to be beautiful. *You* are designed to be beautiful.

Not *Cosmopolitan* beautiful—that demands perfect proportions, symmetrical features and flawless skin. Magazine beauty is superficial beauty, an attractiveness that's only millimetres deep, and few of us were designed for that. Our noses are bent, our hair lacks shine, our wobbly bits are, well, a little too wobbly. For most of us, 21st-century western ideals of loveliness are out of our grasp.

Real beauty—that's what we were designed for. We were made for the kind of beauty that starts in the heart and overflows into every part of our being. It's a beauty that is utterly captivating, precious beyond measure, and deep; so deep that it's foundational to everything we say and do. It's the kind of beauty that flows from utter fulfilment, complete contentment, a purposeful life and a sense of security about who we are.

It's a beauty that no one can manufacture for themselves but which is instantly obvious and overwhelmingly alluring when it comes into view. It's an attractiveness that has absolutely nothing to do with how we look on the outside and everything to do with how we are on the inside. It's a quality that makes you smile whenever you see it. That's what we are made to enjoy.

Not just stopping

I was discussing this book with my hairdresser recently. My hairdresser has a wonderful way of speaking her mind. "So basically," she said, "your book's about sexual fantasies and pornography, and you're going to say: *That's stupid, stop it, don't do it anymore*". I pondered her words for a while (I had some time, the blow-drier was far too loud for an instant response). Was that all my book was going to say? *Stop it?!*

No.

"It's about starting, not stopping," I eventually replied. "It's about becoming something, or someone; about becoming the attractive women that we are made to be."

And that means becoming more and more like Jesus, by enjoying knowing him more and more.

That might not be what you were expecting. I guess you may have picked up this book because you want to stop struggling with sexual fantasies or because you've got a friend who's trapped in the web of pornography use and you want to help them give up their addiction. Maybe you're expecting the tone of this book to be negative: "It's important to change your awful ways". Maybe you were expecting the message to be very practical: "Here are six steps to defeating the grip of porn".

That's not how it's going to be. Because neither really works. In the coming chapters we'll be talking about things that aren't beautiful. We'll be being honest about the murky world of our minds and the impact of pornography on every facet of our lives. But the real aim, the ultimate goal, of these pages is to encourage you to become more like Jesus, the perfect embodiment of true attractiveness. We'll be setting aside the world's lies about loveliness, and pursuing a complete reorientation of our beings so we can enjoy the fruit of deep-down beauty. My hope is that this will be an exciting, liberating and positive journey to take.

So take a moment to reflect: Can you imagine yourself having a true, soul-deep beauty? Does it seem possible that you could become that kind of woman... or does it feel unobtainable, unrealistic, maybe even unpalatable? It can be hard to imagine ourselves in that light when we know just what are minds are capable of right now, but change is possible.

But change is rarely easy. So let's capture the vision of what this life of real beauty looks like, so that we want, more than anything, to experience it.

Beautiful or boring?

I asked a few of my Christian friends what they thought their lives might look like if they were living a truly beautiful Christian life now. One thought about the image of a nun: someone who spends hours in prayer and contemplation, knows the Bible backwards, and goes about doing good works during the day before retreating to solitude at night. Another painted a picture of a stereotypical missionary, who spent their waking hours wandering from village to village doing evangelistic talks and developing callouses on their knees from fervent praying.

There is an element of truth in those scenarios. But my friends' conceptions of a beautiful Christian were ones where there was no time to enjoy God's world, no time for relationships, no time for sex or child-bearing, no time for laughter (or any other emotion for that matter). When they thought of a beautiful Christian life, they thought of a dull life.

And that is not what a beautiful life, or a good life, looks like.

Beautiful image

The beginning of the world was wonderful. In the first two chapters of the Bible, as the creation events unfold, every word drips with delight. As God brought into being seas and stars, fish and birds, his repeated verdict was: "It is good". As he brought everything into being, he was very pleased with what he had made. And he was right to be—the world is astonishing. The stunning views, the mind-blowing sunsets, the delicacy of tiny flowers, the power of the wind, the complexity of the nervous system, the humour of the duck-billed platypus... Few hearts remain unmoved by the diversity and artistry of God's handiwork.

But none of that was the best bit—no sunrise or petal brought God as much pleasure as what came next. The highlight, the absolute pinnacle of creation, was us. When God made people, his work that day wasn't just good; it was "very good" (Genesis 1 v 31). The man and woman God made weren't just animals with larger brains and a greater capacity for communication: "God created mankind in his own image ... male and female he created them" (v 27). We are little images of God himself. We are designed to relate to God and to one another in ways that are supremely intimate and unswervingly loving, because that's how God wants to relate to us. We are designed to look after the world carefully and generously, because that's how God rules his creation.

We don't live in that world now—it has been spoiled by humanity. But when we cry for more than this world seems to offer… when we sense that we need more than this world says will satisfy us… we are right. We were made beautiful, in God's image. We were made for perfection.

There's great value in being a human being. And there's great beauty in great value. It's truly beautiful.

Beautiful relationships

The relationships in that world were truly beautiful, too. Right from the start, God said that it wasn't good for a human being to be alone. It's impossible to live a good and full life in isolation. That's why God made men and women—to complement one another, to be community together.

And the relationship between the first man and woman was wonderful. When the Bible describes their relationship, it says simply:

> *Adam and his wife were both naked, and they felt no shame. (Genesis 2 v 25)*

It's hardly a full account of their marriage! But think about what it shows us: here was a relationship characterised by intimacy,   concerns to be avoided.

There are no relationships this good in this broken world. But we can enjoy relationships that come close, at least at times.

That doesn't mean we have to have a husband or boyfriend for life to be bearable—singleness is a gift from God that is in no way a second-class life. We don't have to be in a romantic relationship to be complete, and we can be satisfied without sex. But a beautiful life is one where there are significant relationships of great depth to be enjoyed.

After all, God is a relational God—he is Father, Son and Spirit. And you are made in his image. So a beautiful life will mean relating to others; will mean giving and receiving love. We are designed for relationships. We simply cannot live as God wants and as, deep down, we want, unless we are in community.

Beautiful life

Here is a wonderful, deeply beautiful life. A life of great dignity, real love, complete security and total trust. But as we've said, we don't live in that world. Where is that life to be found today?

I suppose everything I've written so far could be summed up in one simple sentence. A beautiful life is one that is centred on Christ and the work he did on the cross. When Jesus was on earth, he said something beautifully simple:

> *I have come that they may have life, and have it to the full. (John 10 v 10)*

A full life—a life that is ever more beautiful, satisfying and enjoyable—is what Jesus, the Son of God, came to offer you and me. Just as those first humans knew a life of beauty because it was lived with God, so we know that life as we live with Jesus, the God-man.

In the verses that follow, Jesus goes on to explain that this wonderful, purposeful life comes through him laying down his life for us.

So if we want to pursue an ever more beautiful life, we need to be clear from the start that we can't do it without knowing Jesus. He is the place where beauty is seen, offered and enjoyed. You might be someone who indulges in the occasional sexual fantasy, or someone who has an addiction to internet pornography that overtakes you every day, or someone who is somewhere between those two.

Whoever you are, you cannot fix this by yourself. You might kick the porn habit. You might shut down the fantasising for a while. But that won't make you beautiful, deep down inside. That won't change your heart, and its inbuilt tendency to ignore God and love what is second-rate or worse. On your own, you'll end up exhausted, disillusioned or defeated.

But with Jesus—loving him, knowing we're loved by him, and seeking to live his way—things can be different; things can change; a beautiful purity is possible; we can become the people that, deep down, most of us want to be.

Beautiful isn't easy

Becoming this kind of beautiful isn't easy. It means swimming against the tide of our society, which sees a "full life" as a life that grabs sexual experience in whatever form looks good and feels right. It will mean working against the misguided desires of your own heart. It's hard to live beautifully.

But the question is: what kind of woman would you like to be? Do you want to give in to your instincts on a whim? Do you want to cover up the pain of the past or the longings of the present with some cheap sex-substitute? Or do you want a life where your mind, your heart, your mouth and your body are in step with the Spirit of God and bringing glory to Jesus? Do you want to experience a pure life, without regrets and the desperation of settling for second best? Do you want a life of contentment, of value and of peace?

The possibility of deep beauty is real and it's truly wonderful. The more you experience it, the more you want it. And the tragedy is that, when we seek to feel beautiful in our fantasies, we walk further and further from beauty—we become less and less the people we'd like to be. It's to those people—the people we are right now—that we turn next. That will be less pleasant. But as we do it, keep your eyes fixed on the person you can become. You were designed to be beautiful. And, through Jesus, you can be that woman.

2. Fantasy

Liz crashed into bed. She was alone again. It had been one of those evenings. There was this guy she'd liked. Great eyes, wonderful sense of humour; one of those people who makes you feel you're the most important person in the universe when he speaks to you. When they first started talking, she wondered if there might be potential. It's not that she was desperate for romance, but the thought of having a new man around had its appeal.

But then he dropped the bombshell: "My wife and I are just back from Brazil".

Your wife? You have a wife?!

She didn't hear a word of his tales of South America. She was livid. He gave her a glimmer of hope and then cruelly snatched it away. How dare he?

She made her excuses, circulated among other friends at the party for a bit, and then went home. Her eyes welled up. "How could I have been so stupid? As if anyone would ever want me."

And then it dawned on her. He may be off-limits in the real world… but not in her mind. The next hour was lost in a swirl of explicit fantasy. A fantasy that recurred for the next three weeks.

Sound familiar? Or maybe this next scenario is more you?

Kate was alone. Everyone else was out; no one else could see, but she drew the curtains anyway, enclosing herself in a cocoon in which to keep her secret safe. It had been a tough day: she had been fighting deadlines at work, she was irritated with a friend, and she needed to go out in an hour to a meeting that she resented having to attend. She was stressed, and she had no one to talk to.

She needed to relax. She wanted a hug. In the real world, neither of those things seemed possible.

But there was a place online that offered some respite.

She started to type. Moments later, pornhub appeared. An image caught her eye and she clicked on the link. For a while, the world seemed a better place.

But not for long. She glanced at her clock and her heart started to pound. She was late for that meeting. Her mind started to race. What was she doing? Moments before, she had been lost in a web of sexual intrigue… and now she was about to go to a church event. What a hypocrite! How could she live like this

*week after week? Guilt swept over her, but she sup-
pressed it quickly. She needed to put on a front.*

*So she freshened up, grabbed her Bible, and left for
her pastor's house.*

Feeling new

Fantasy, erotica and pornography—the sexual fiction we
imagine, read or watch—take us out of this world and
transport us to a whole new dimension. For a few minutes (or
a few hours) the reality of this life seems a million miles away.

We can pretend to be anything we like.

The lonely become popular. No longer ignored by colleagues
and neighbours, we can imagine ourselves at the centre
of the room. Friends hang on our every word. The kind of
people who wouldn't give us a second glance in real life find
us irresistible. The pain of living with no physical contact is
replaced by massage and more.

The ugly become desirable. No crooked teeth, bulging waistlines
or unsightly scars get in the way of cyber-sex. No potential
partner looks through us to the gorgeous brunette standing a
foot away. Their eyes meet ours and they are entranced.

The unfulfilled become satisfied. No more faking it with
our husband. No more pretending to be aroused when the
reality is we feel as sensual as a box of cereal. We can be in the
moment with someone who caters for our every whim. We
can feel everything we want to feel.

The curious become enlightened. Those scenarios that
we just don't want to suggest, or those scenarios that we
have no one to suggest to, are no longer out of reach. Our
preferences can be explored, our ideas enjoyed. Everything

is great in our fantasy world.

The abused become strong. Daily life might involve, or have involved, acting as someone's punch-bag, but in our world, our inner world, we are dominant, safe… maybe even wreaking some revenge.

In our minds, we temporarily recreate the world as we would like it to be. It helps us feel in control; it makes us feel new. And that is no small matter.

Feeling great

I don't for one moment want to glorify pornography, but let's be honest: feeling new feels good. Actually, it feels *great*. Who doesn't want to be part of a scenario where our wildest dreams come true, in a fantasy where we are in charge and everyone around us is pandering to our every desire?

There are no limits to who we can be, what we can try or who else can be there. We're surrounded by other people, but immune from getting hurt (unless, of course, that is what we are seeking). In fantasy-land, no one says no to us; everyone is keen to jump to our agenda; and that feels wonderful.

And it's not just our mind that gets aroused—our body joins in too. Endorphins, the body's pleasure-inducing hormones, are released, promoting an extraordinary sense of well being that everyone enjoys.

I remember reading my first erotic novel. I was 17 and had a Saturday job in a public library. One afternoon as I was re-shelving the returns, I picked an item at random and signed it out in my name. I didn't bother reading the back cover—I was simply familiarising myself with the stock, and so I had no idea what I was carrying in my bag.

Back in my room, at home, I began to turn the pages. A wave of language I'd never seen before hit me as scenarios that had never crossed my mind were introduced to my imagination. Every movement and every sensation the characters experienced was described in graphic detail; and I was hooked. I liked reading most books. I *loved* reading this one.

Why? Because it didn't just inform me or inspire me. It transported me. The power of the language was so strong that I didn't merely feel for the characters; I felt what they felt. And I liked it. I liked it a lot.

But that feeling didn't last.

Feeling alone

If you've ever used pornography, read erotica or constructed an explicit fantasy in your mind, you'll know what I'm talking about. The pleasure goes up and up… and then comes crashing down. Far from the lingering, relaxed comfort that sex with a loving husband brings, arousal from fantasy is short-lived and hollow.

The problem is this. When the chapter is over, the fantasy complete or the video-clip ended, you look around and are confronted with one inescapable fact:

I am on my own.

All those people who were attending to you, that special someone who was making you feel so good in your mind's eye—they're not real. There is no one pandering to your every whim. The person who you imagined being intimate with isn't in the room, and hasn't got a clue you are thinking of them in that way. Everything that has just flown through your imagination has been fake.

In a few short seconds, you go from being in the arms of your ideal partner to sitting in solitary confinement. You come down to reality with a thud.

And that makes everything worse. The lonely feel lonelier, the ugly feel uglier, the unfulfilled feel tossed aside, the curious are no closer to their dreams and the abused become weaker still. The fleeting fancy that offered so much disappears in a moment and leaves us utterly isolated.

To make matters even worse, it feels as if there is no one we can turn to. How would a conversation asking for help even begin? "I've just spent the last hour watching strangers make each other scream with ecstasy, and I'm feeling a bit low as a result—can I come round for a cuppa?"

And so we imagine that we're the only people in the world struggling like this. We convince ourselves that all our friends are sorted, self-controlled and sexually sane. We tell ourselves that we are the odd ones out. Never mind that female use of pornography is growing fast and sales of erotica are going through the roof; we believe it's only us that struggle.

I think all this is even worse for Christians. The Bible speaks so clearly of the need for sexual purity, and we imagine that our female friends are living up to that standard. We think their thoughts are pure. We think that their marriages are stress-free. We think their frustrations are limited to traffic queues and work deadlines. It doesn't even occur to us that they might be hitting the porn shortcut on their mobile phones too.

Feeling out of control

It's a vicious circle. The lonelier we get, the more we seek the consolation of fantasy. The more we seek fantasy, the lonelier we become. Each moment of engagement with explicit material takes us a step further down the spiral—but there's nowhere else to go.

Then, one day (and not all of us are at this stage) we discover that pornography and fantasy are no longer a choice—they are a compulsion. They own us. We are a solitary puppet on the string of lust.

There may be days, even weeks, of self-control—but the temptation, the "need" to watch one more clip, read one more chapter, just to help us on a bad day, kicks in. The draw seems irresistible and we cave in.

For women who reach this point, life is well and truly out of control. Illness is feigned so that solid time can be spent in front of the screen instead of going to work. Housework, studies or social activities get dropped to allow space to indulge the next phase of the fantasy. Sleep-deprivation is seen as an acceptable trade-off for momentary pleasures, and our lives spiral out of control.

Most women reading this book aren't at this stage. And you can't imagine it getting like this for you. But that's the point— no one imagines themselves becoming this kind of woman, until it happens. Complacency smooths our descent to this place of virtual addiction.

Anna was a porn addict. She knows firsthand how ensnaring the web can be. It started as intrigue: her marriage was on the rocks because her husband had been having an affair. He'd come clean, repented and changed—but Anna was angry. As a Christian, she had only ever slept with him, and only once they were married. But after the affair she was tormented

*with the idea that he was now far more sexually
experienced than her. He had engaged in intercourse
in places that she had never dreamed of and she felt
sick at her own naivety. So she went online.*

*Initially it was just a clip. She'd hit play on a short
video and watch a few seconds. But it wasn't long
before she wanted more and more. The clips got
longer; the material became darker. She investigated
anything that she felt would give her the upper hand
in their marriage. She "needed" to turn the tables.
She yearned to feel that she had done things that her
husband hadn't.*

*It didn't help. No scenario was ever enough to satisfy
her desire for revenge; but that didn't stop her looking. Soon it was porn every morning before work,
porn every lunchtime at work. Hidden in a cubicle
in the ladies' toilet, she would hit play "just one more
time". She was trapped and disgusted at what she
had become. But she carried on anyway.*

Feeling dirty

Disgusted. That's the word I hear most often when talking
with women about their engagement with sexually explicit
material. We feel dirty, tainted, just plain bad.

Why? Some in 21st-century western society tell us that our
Christian beliefs cause us to suppress our desires and then
programme us to feel guilt when we unleash them.

But I didn't grow up in a Christian household. Nor was I
ever told that sex is bad. Many other women who feel guilt

at their use of porn weren't, either. If religion is to blame for the guilt, you'd think the guilt would get less in our post-Christian society. But it hasn't. We may suppress it, hide it, or try to ignore it, but it's still there. Why? Might it be that, deep down, we know that the life of fantasy is not the life we are designed to live? That we have an idea, possibly unspoken, that our porn and fantasy use is getting in the way of the true beauty we were designed to exhibit? And so we dislike ourselves—sometimes we hate ourselves—for what we've done to ourselves.

But the dirt contaminates more than just our opinion of ourselves. It infects our relationship with other people too. When we fantasise or use porn, we begin to see others as objects rather than precious bearers of God's image. People become tools that exist to give us what we desire.

Our expectations of how others should treat us and how we should treat them become skewed. We forget that the people on the screens are acting, sometimes under duress, and that the characters on the pages of our books or in our minds are fictional. They aren't really getting wonderfully aroused by what's happening to them. It's fake—so fake that pornography sets employ "fluffers", people paid to keep the actors aroused. Orgasms are frequently faked on screen. The scenarios set out in books are unrealistic in the extreme. But we forget all that as we buy into the lie. And then when, in real life, people don't live up to the fiction, we become resentful and dissatisfied. Relationships fall apart. New ones become more difficult to form. Our inner lives and outer lives gradually begin to crumble.

And then there's our relationship with God. It's so hard to talk to him after watching porn or retreating into our imaginary world. We know we've done something that he doesn't like. We know we've devalued a precious gift and, like a small child who has disobeyed their parent, we try to avoid his gaze. Soaked in disgust, we assume that God would want nothing to do with us now. Forgiveness is not for people like us.

> *Mel loved Jesus very much. She went to church every Sunday, had a time of Bible-reading and prayer every morning and was active in providing meals for the homeless. She was also addicted to an inner fantasy-world.*
>
> *Meticulously constructed over a period of years, she had created a whole new existence for herself: a set of fictional friends, who met for fictional conversations. Much of it was far from erotic—just some girls chatting over coffee. But at the end of every daydream, she took one particular girl back to her place. There the intimacy began.*
>
> *Her fantasies got more adventurous and explicit as the months went on. She told herself that no one was getting hurt, and justified it to herself as an attempt to rationalise the same-sex attraction she was experiencing without actually involving another woman. She pretended everything was fine, but she noticed a trend. After she came back from her fictional world, she couldn't pick up her Bible; she couldn't face speaking to anyone from church. Fantasy erected a barrier in her mind, and she responded by trying to hide from God.*

Do you recognise any of those feelings of dirtiness? Plenty of women do. Shocked and appalled at our grubby behaviour, we resolve never to indulge in such thinking again. But we do, and the mess gets messier.

Which raises the question: "Why?" Why would any rational, intelligent human being choose to live this way? Why would I keep doing what gives me such a shallow, passing high and such a deep, lasting low?

There may have been many circumstances that have nudged us towards porn-use or escaping into fantasy. Some of those circumstances may have been desperately painful. And they should never be minimised. But underneath all those things lies the true answer to the "Why?", our biggest problem of all: our hearts.

3. Reality

I vividly remember the first time I saw a human heart. Brown, squishy and inanimate, it made quite an impression on my mind. I was in an anatomy class, enthralled by the process of matching up things I'd read about with the specimen before me and largely unaware of the mass nausea all around. But alongside the thrill of spotting arteries and valves, I remember a sobering moment: what I was holding in my hand hadn't always been an object of scientific interest. Once, it had been the very driving force of a life.

The Bible uses the word "heart" a lot; but when it speaks of the heart, it isn't referring to the pump that keeps our blood flowing freely; it is speaking of our driving force. It's talking about our inner being, our very self, the place from where our hopes, dreams, desires and priorities flow. My heart is the real me.

When God is at work in his people, much of what flows from the human heart can be wonderful. From our hearts we love our Saviour, we love our family, our church, our neighbours and even our enemies. From our hearts we long to taste the wonder of the world that God has made. From our hearts comes the passion to help others get to know Jesus.

But in its natural state, the human heart is not a pure place. Indeed, the prophet Jeremiah made an astonishingly bleak assessment:

> *The heart is deceitful above all things and beyond cure.*
> *(Jeremiah 17 v 9)*

It can be easy to get a bit defensive when it comes to Jeremiah. As I read his accusation, I sometimes feel like shouting: "You lived 2,500 years ago. You didn't know me. How dare you make a judgment about my heart?" But the problem is that Scripture isn't ultimately Jeremiah's words. It's God's word, and there's no getting away from the reality: God lives today, he knows me all too well, and he, more than anyone else can make an assessment of the state of my heart. And he says it is deceitful. If I look inside myself, I can see it's true. I think you can, too.

Which means that this chapter isn't an easy one for me to write, and won't be for you to read.

What our hearts make

When we're honest, we know that the things we desire, the things we want to possess or experience aren't always, or even often, pure. Rather than being satisfied with the opportunity to enjoy God's gifts of money, relationships and responsibility, our hearts start to hunt wealth, people and power. They take good things and turn them into god things. Our hearts make things God has made into idols.

There are many different types of idols. Some of them are blatant. Throughout the Bible, there are examples of people doing what Paul describes as exchanging: "the glory of the immortal God for images made to look like a mortal human being and birds and animals and reptiles" (Romans 1 v 23). When he visited Athens, Paul was confronted with a city full of the things (Acts 17 v 16-34). Whether you wanted wealth, health or fertility, there was a shrine to visit. In street after street there were lumps of gold or stone pretending to be gods. They offered a better life—more money, healthier crops, extra children for you (or your ox)—but, being inanimate objects, they didn't actually come up with the goods. You could leave as many offerings as you liked at their feet, but they never made your life better.

Some idols aren't quite as easy to see as the 18-breasted statues or stone animals of the ancient world. An idol is anything that we believe will give us a better life, and which we give things to and give things up for in order to gain that life. My heart doesn't need someone to make a statue for me to worship an idol. It's quite capable of manufacturing a variety of idols for me to love instead of God. The 16th-century reformer, John Calvin, described the human heart as an "idol-factory", and he was right.

And as we live for our idols, they lead to all kinds of behaviours that dishonour God. Paul fleshes this out for us in his letter to the Ephesians:

> *But among you there must not be even a hint of sexual immorality, or of any kind of impurity, or of greed, because these are improper for God's holy people. Nor should there be obscenity, foolish talk or coarse joking, which are out of place, but rather thanksgiving. For of this you can be sure: no immoral, impure or*

> *greedy person—such a person is an idolater—has any*
> *inheritance in the kingdom of Christ and of God.*
> *(Ephesians 5 v 3-5)*

It can be easy to gloss over verses like this and convince ourselves that because we haven't cracked any dirty jokes this week or slept around, we're doing OK. But if we are involved in pornography, we have been sexually immoral in the way we use our eyes; if we have explicit fantasies, we have been entertaining obscenity in our minds. These verses are talking about us. And they show us that our thoughts and actions aren't just a random occurrence or a product of our environment. They are driven by a misplaced longing deep within us that we are choosing to follow instead of God.

Ungodly behaviour stems from ungodly worship—it's as simple as that. If we want money more than God, our behaviour will show a drive for things that outstrips any drive for holiness. If we want a man more than we want to be faithful to God, we will act in ways that pursue relationships with other people (real or fictional), and let our relationship with God slip into the sidelines. It's cause and effect.

She had it all...

The story of Eve in the Garden of Eden illustrates just how our inner idols work. Eve was in a perfect place, in a perfect relationship with God and with a perfect man by her side. No woman has ever had it better than Eve had it in Genesis 2.

There was only one "no" in Eve's perfect world. She must not eat the fruit from the tree of the knowledge of good and evil. Why? Because it represented rule—and the throne of the world is a place for God alone. God had warned that if she disobeyed and ate it, she would "certainly die" (Genesis 2 v 17).

She has it all… and she loses it all. Why? Because the devil, in the form of a snake, sidles up to her and, when she explains God's warning, responds:

> *You will not certainly die … God knows that when you eat from it your eyes will be opened, and you will be like God, knowing good and evil. (Genesis 3 v 4-5)*

So the woman starts to look at this forbidden fruit:

> *When [she] saw that the fruit of the tree was good for food and pleasing to the eye, and also desirable for gaining wisdom, she took some and ate it. (v 6)*

It's not enough for the devil to convince the woman that God won't carry out the punishment of death for her disobedience. He also has to get her to *want* to disobey. So he offers her some idols. And the woman worships them. She wants the experience of tasting the "pleasing" forbidden fruit more than she wants to be faithful. She wants the knowledge the fruit would bring more than she wants to trust God's good plans. She wants to control her own life more than she wants to submit to God's will, even though he has given her utter perfection. She reaches out for the idols of experience, knowledge and control. She eats the fruit.

As she eats, she gets everything she wanted. And she loses everything that matters. Within 17 verses, she experiences separation from God, tension with her partner, and the alienation of the world that had been made for her.

What's all this got to do with porn and fantasy? Simply this.

God says that sex outside marriage is sexual immorality—it is disobedience. So when we are tempted to watch, read or imagine that kind of sex, we are facing the same temptation the first woman did. We are being offered an idol, and—as we turn on the computer, open the book or close our eyes to escape to our make-believe world—we are choosing to believe the lie that that idol will give us everything we want.

The idols of our heart take a natural desire for a man, and twist it so we end up convincing ourselves that life is meaningless without a husband; so much so that, if there isn't a real husband around, we need to invent a fake partner. Or they take the normal desire to want to experience new things, and twist it so we convince ourselves that unless we have some specific experience in life—like satisfying sex—there is no way we can ever be complete or fulfilled; and so, in the absence of great sex in the real world, we opt for exciting cyber-sex instead. They whisper in our ear: *You deserve more than God has given you. You need more than he has chosen to bless you with. You need me. I can give you it all.*

But we can leave as many offerings as we like at our idols' feet; they never make our lives better. We believe their hollow promises, we give up our purity to grab some fake sexual experiences... and then we discover that, just like the lumps of metal in Athens, they bring nothing that lasts except regret. They are grim, disappointing liars.

If our idols were statues on street corners, they would be easy to spot. The idols in our hearts are harder to identify. They're happy for us to worship them without really realising what we're doing. We tend to be much better at recognising the idols of other cultures and other people than our own.

But make no mistake, they're there. In the next chapter, we're going to take a tour of our own hearts.

4. Factory

My heart is an idol-factory. That's the sad reality. All our hearts are. And when it comes to manufacturing idols, there is an almost infinite number of different fake gods that our factories produce. But there are three idols that I seem to see in my life—and in the lives of the women I know—more than any others: relationships, experience and control. These are idols that most of us seem to make in our hearts.

The idol of relationships
The early church in Corinth was a messed-up place. The married people wanted to be single, and the single people wanted to be married. The letter Paul wrote to these wayward brothers and sisters makes for some challenging reading, and there are two verses in 1 Corinthians 7 that pack a particular punch.

First, Paul points out that both marriage and singleness are wonderful examples of God's lavish generosity:

> *I wish that all of you were as I am. But each of you has your own gift from God; one has this gift, another has that. (1 Corinthians 7 v 7)*

If you are married, your husband is a gift from God. If you are single, your singleness is a gift from God. And God does not give bad gifts! Both marriage and singleness are gifts; neither is better.

Scripture says it's good to be single. Trouble is, not many people around us feel or act as though that's true—including within our churches—and it's easy to get sucked in.

So the idol of relationships is a big one in our society. It's the whisper in our hearts that if life is to be full and meaningful, we need a man.

And it's a whisper we're naturally ready to listen to. Very few little girls dream of being an old spinster. Very few Hollywood blockbusters celebrate contented singleness. We live in a world where 40-year-old virgins are ridiculed, and culture constantly peddles the idea that you need a man to "Complete Me" (as the chick-flick title puts it). To worship the idol of relationships is normal. But it's not biblical; and it's not helpful.

Every woman, consciously or subconsciously, asks herself the question: *If God chooses to give me his gift of singleness long-term, or for life, will I accept that gift as something good?* If the answer is no, we will set up the idol of relationships in our heart. We may love God, but we will love the idea of being with a man more. We will feel dissatisfied with God's generosity; we will feel unfulfilled; we will long for human intimacy more than we long to be the woman God has designed us to be.

And more often than not, we will act on those longings. For some of us it will involve getting into a relationship with someone unsuitable. For many more, it will mean fleeing the painful reality of singleness in this world by creating a fantasy or online world where our dreams can be partially fulfilled.

After all, no one need know about that. No one will raise their eyebrows about it. And it dulls the pain… at least for a while.

Single women often assume that, once you're dating or married, this idol says a polite goodbye and quietly vacates your heart. It doesn't. Where single women idolise having a husband, a married woman very easily idolises having a different husband. They can convince themselves they've chosen the wrong person; they can long for someone more tender, more caring, more attentive, more generous. They can start to imagine what it would be like to have an upgraded husband or a completely different one. Before long, it's easy to want an ideal relationship more than to honour God through a faithful marriage. Some opt for an affair; some walk away. Others stay in the marriage, but pursue their idol of relationships in fantasy-land, where the partner of their dreams sits waiting, doting on their every word. After all, no one need know about that…

The idol of experience

In the James Bond film *The World Is Not Enough*, the main villain, Renard, and his lover, Elektra King, share a catch-phrase that resonates around the western world:

> *"There's no point in living, if you can't feel alive."*

Our 21st-century culture is obsessed with self-fulfilment. We want to find ourselves, reach our potential, live our dreams. Missing out is the worst thing that can happen to anyone. Even if, as Christians, we know Jesus is supreme, we often live our lives as though our ambitions and aspirations were central.

I'm an experience junkie. I love to try new things. I'm not a complete adrenalin seeker (I will probably manage to get through my life quite happily without jumping out of a plane) but in most aspects of my life, I like to feel as though I've given things a go. If a new shop or theatre opens, I want to visit it. If a new restaurant appears, I want to taste the food. If there's a chance to feed a tiger cub, try a new type of dancing or learn a new skill, I'm in. It's called having a zest for life, and there's nothing wrong with that—unless, of course, my love of experience outgrows my love of God. Then I'm into idol territory.

God has placed us in a wonderful world, and it's great to explore that world and express our innate creativity which stems from being made in God's image; but we need to have a safety valve in our mind. As well as being able to say: "I'd love to give that a go", we need to be able to say: "It's OK if I don't experience that". We'll only say that if we remember that, however exciting or unique that experience would be, it cannot match knowing Christ and his love. If that safety valve fails, we're in trouble.

This is never more true than when it comes to sex.

One of the hardest things about singleness is celibacy. Many can cope with earning money, doing all the household chores and making decisions without a husband, but never having sex is a real challenge. And—we're all women here— for many of us, there are certain times of the month when it is considerably more of a challenge than at others. Our bodies scream for what is not available, and all too often our minds listen to our hormonal cry for stimulation more than our spiritual need for purity.

For some single women, the idol of experience can be an extension of natural curiosity. Most women want to know what sex looks like and feels like—that's normal. However, if we can't say: "I accept that I may never know" instead of insisting: "I want to know now", the idol of experience has reared its head again. The drive to see, to touch and to experience overtakes the desire to honour God, and we head to fantasy-land or the internet for a tainted glimpse of what we may—or may not—one day experience for real.

Women who are happily dating often feel they are on the road to marriage. As they fall deeper and deeper in love with the man they want to be faithful to, they crave greater intimacy, This is perfectly natural too. But if that desire for physical unity overtakes the desire to please the King of the universe, the idol risks leading even the most self-controlled woman's mind into a murky world of sordid fantasy. Dating does not come with a promise of marriage. So our fantasy is not real—it is not necessarily our future. And, of course, the danger of a fantasy is that we can end up making it reality, way before a wedding.

Again, marriage is no protection from idolatry. No marriages are perfect and no couple has a perfect sex life all the time—exhaustion-induced, unsatisfying sex is no reason to push the panic button, and not every good marriage includes great sex. But marriages that are seriously on the rocks can be as celibate as any singleness, and marriages that are dysfunctional can, sometimes, revolve around repeated, unsatisfying, sexual encounters. These are fertile ground for the idol of experience to grow in.

Some married women I've spoken to talk of, at best, "faking it" over a period of decades or, at worst, consistently enduring positions that are pure pain, not pleasure. And so it's very easy to give up on our marriages—mentally at least. We convince ourselves that "it's over" with our husband, and decide to pursue the experience of sexual fulfilment without him. We convince ourselves that married people deserve good sex; if we can't get it in our marriage, we're within our rights to go elsewhere. We may not go as far as having an affair, but we still want the fulfilment. The high of sexual climax becomes more important than the relationship in which it was designed to be enjoyed; the idol of experience kicks in and pornography, erotica or fantasy gain a foothold.

Siobhan had a plan for her life. She even had a list. Degree by 21, married by 25, mother by 27. 17 countries to be visited by the time the kids come along. Northern Lights viewed, mountains climbed, capital cities visited. The trouble was, when 30 came, she was still single. No one had uttered those four magic words: "Will you marry me?" Celibacy wasn't part of the plan. Things had gone wrong. She wasn't living the life that she was designed to live.

So she decided to compensate. She got out a notebook and wrote down in lurid detail all the sexual exploits she wanted to have experienced by now. And each night she re-read her fantasies—she tasted for a few short moments life as it "should" be.

A word about same-sex attraction

One experience that the Bible says is definitely off-limits to those who are following the all-loving, all-wise God is any kind of homosexual encounter. God's word says of a fallen world:

> *Even their women exchanged natural sexual relations*
> *for unnatural ones. In the same way the men also*
> *abandoned natural relations with women and were*
> *inflamed with lust for one another. Men committed*
> *shameful acts with other men, and received in*
> *themselves the due penalty for their error.*
>
> *(Romans 1 v 26-27)*

These are uncomfortable words, and those of us (and I do mean *us*) who have experienced fleeting or persistent thoughts of same-sex attraction will know how overwhelmingly crushing it can be to be confronted with the fact that God says it's best for us never to act on those inclinations. The form of sex that feels as though it is going to be the most natural and the most fulfilling is, permanently, off-limits. How many tears have been shed, how many pillows punched at the seemingly callous injustice of such a restriction?

Some people respond by rejecting God completely, shunning a relationship with their Creator in order to follow their heart's desire. Others re-write God—they say that he's changed his mind since the Bible was written, or maybe wasn't guiding the words of the biblical authors very carefully when they penned their books; so he actually doesn't really mind what consenting, adult women do between the sheets.

Those of us who know God to be good, loving and sovereign can't usually bring ourselves to go down those routes—outright denial of our Lord is inconceivable—but despite our outward willingness to accept God's will, we often continue to hold the idol of lesbian experience close. We kid ourselves that looking lustfully at another woman on screen to satisfy our inner desires isn't too bad. We talk about the joy of singleness while secretly imagining the woman of our dreams. We might read lesbian literature to indulge fleetingly in a moment of "if onlys". And when we do, we are faced with the inescapable conclusion that our idol is getting the upper hand—we're believing the lie that a spot of same-sex fantasy will give us something better than God ever could.

The idol of control

Pain hurts. Not my most profound statement, I know, but true. If you have opened your heart to someone and they have wounded you, you will know exactly what I am talking about. And once it's happened, many of us are keen to ensure that it never happens again. There's nothing intrinsically wrong with wanting safety—God encourages us to run to him for protection. A Christian can enjoy knowing:

> *The LORD is my rock, my fortress and my deliverer; my God is my rock, in whom I take refuge, my shield and the horn of my salvation, my stronghold.*
>
> *(Psalm 18 v 2)*

But if, instead of running to God, we try to create our own safe world—if the only Rock we'll lean on and trust is ourselves—then idolatry has raised its head once more.

And making a world where you're in control is very tempting if your heart has been broken or you've been abused, and you never want to feel that pain again; or if in the real world you are in a relationship where you have little or no say in the bedroom; or at times when everything else—work, church, parenting—all seem to be spiralling out of control.

In a world that can so often seem so out of our control, a fantasy where we call the shots is extremely attractive. And that's what the idol of control offers.

Ali had survived an awful childhood. Rejected by her parents, fostered by a family where the uncle was a paedophile, she was simultaneously repulsed by and resigned to regular sex by the time she was 12. She complied as a teenager. She complied every week until she was rescued aged 15 and social services found her a new place to live.

Working through the pain with her counsellor was awful. Coming to terms with the loss of her inno-cence amid such violence took years. It was difficult to imagine what a loving Father could really be like. But, with Jesus as her ultimate Saviour, she started to love and trust again.

But there was one area of her life where she wouldn't budge. She was never going to let any man tell her what to do, ever again. It was her life and she was going to live it in charge of the men around her. She became dominant in her relationships at work. She became dominant in the bedroom. And she loved to view clips of female dominance on screen. Any image of women inflicting pain on men brought a sense of justice and stability to her hurting mind.

This idol promises us so much. But the trouble is, when our desire for safety and security over-rides our desire to be the beautiful woman God wants us to be, we either start to manipulate people in the real world, or we construct a fantasy world (online, on the page or in our heads) where we define how our relationships work and where we set the moral parameters, not the Lord. That's the idol of control at play. That idol, maybe more than any other, drives us back to a world of tainted possibilities on the web or in our heads.

Destination diagnosis

It might be that you've spotted your idol(s) already. Sometimes they don't lurk very deep. If you're wondering, mine's control. What's yours?

If you're not sure, try asking yourself these questions:

1. Are you pleased that God has given you your gift of singleness/marriage, or do you think your life would be better if your circumstances were to change?
   The latter points to the idol of relationships.

2. Are you content to wait to experience sex (if you are single), and content to leave some of your dreams unfulfilled (whether single or married)?
   If not, experience-idol may be dragging you away from God.

3. Are you deliberately keeping real people at arm's length to try to avoid getting hurt again? Or worried that the world is a desperately unsafe place to be?
   Then maybe the idol of control is living in you.

5. Guilty

Let me ask you a strange but important question: *Are you more hippo or frog?*

I'm not talking about physical stature (you'll be pleased to know), but about the way you respond to discovering there are idols in your heart. Are you more of a wallower or a jumper?

Hippos are wallowing creatures. If they see a patch of warm, muddy water deep enough to envelop their enormous bodies, they will head for it and sit in it for hours. They snort and they snuffle, they rub and they roll in the filth that surrounds them.

And some of us do that with our idols. We see the things we want more than God—maybe we see them clearly for the first time—and we get overwhelmed by the dirt and rebellion present in our lives. We get hit by a tidal-wave of realisation that we are not the beautiful people God calls us to be, not even the half-beautiful people we thought we were, and we become paralysed by the enormity of who we've become. We wallow. We sit, inert in our sin, shrouded in despair and unable to believe that change is an option.

Frogs, on the other hand, are jumpy creatures. If you sit a frog in some water and turn the heat up slowly, they don't realise, and don't move. But if the heat rises more quickly, they do realise, and they peg it. They have no interest in working out why the water is hot or learning how to avoid dangerous water in the future; they simply hop off as quickly as their powerful back legs can propel them.

Some of us are more like that. When the heat is turned up—when, for whatever reason, we see our idols and our guilt for what they are, when we're confronted with the fact that we have not been living even close to how God desires—we just want to run away from it. We don't actually want to stay and deal with it; we simply want to move to a place where we don't have to think about it anymore.

Most of us have a particular tendency at any given moment in time. And when we allow those tendencies to define our behaviour, we don't change very much. Hippos keep wallowing and frogs keep hopping.

Two fairly extreme examples from the Bible might help us see even more clearly how frogs and hippos operate.

Cain, Eve's eldest son, acted like a frog. He allowed jealousy against his brother to fester to such an extent that he actually killed his brother, Abel. He wanted significance, acceptance and love more than he wanted to be faithful, and his life spiralled out of control as a result. It's a shocking tale of brotherly hatred.

God's response is to ask Cain a question:

Where is your brother Abel? (Genesis 4 v 9)

Cain has a perfect opportunity to admit his sin, confess his idolatry, and ask God for mercy. Instead, he tries to hop away:

Am I my brother's keeper? (v 9)

He might just as well have said: "It's nothing to do with me—let's just move on." He tried to run away from his responsibilities and his past. He failed. And he had to face God's judgment.

Judas, on the other hand, was the ultimate hippo. He had betrayed Jesus to his death for 30 pieces of silver. His idols of power and wealth led him to dump faithfulness in the most heinous way imaginable. He handed over his friend, his leader, his potential Saviour to the authorities to be whipped, mocked, crucified and killed.

He didn't ignore his actions; he was wracked with guilt:

I have sinned ... for I have betrayed innocent blood.
(Matthew 27 v 4)

But he didn't do anything constructive with that guilt. He saw his idolatry in all its ugliness, but instead of running back to God, he wallowed in his self-inflicted filth. Eventually, it killed him:

Judas threw the money into the temple and left. Then he went away and hanged himself. (v 5)

Here is the problem we all face. We are all guilty—none of us meet God's standards. We can try to outrun the guilt—but we cannot outrun God. Or we can own it and face it—but then it will prove a burden too heavy to bear.

Wonderfully, there is a different way—a better way, a God-defined way to deal with idols. First we have to get real about the depth of our rebellion, and then we have to get real about the depth of God's forgiveness. In this chapter and the next, we'll be doing both. We'll be digging into guilt and mercy.

NOT Guilty

Before we do that, however, it's worth taking a moment to reflect on the things about which we don't need to feel guilty. Sometimes we don't feel shame over shameful things. But there are also times when we carry a great load of shame that we have no need to.

1. We don't need to feel guilty about enjoying sex with our husband. Sex is not dirty or bad, nor is it merely a means of having children. There is a whole book of the Bible, Song of Songs, that celebrates the wonderful, loving intimacy of sex with a spouse.

2. We don't need to feel guilty about wanting sex with the person we plan to marry. Song of Songs (in the earlier stages of the book, at least) is an intimate conversation and imagination expressed by two people who are promised to each other but not yet married. They are consistently aware of the dangers of arousing too much intimacy in their relationship (using the repeated refrain: "Do not arouse or awaken love until it so desires" (Song of Songs 2 v 7), but that doesn't stop them longing for each other's bodies. It's great to look forward to sex with the man you have promised to marry.

3. We don't need to feel guilty about liking the idea of being married and having sex one day, even if we don't have a boyfriend right now. Asking God to bring along a godly man with whom to enjoy serving our Saviour is a great prayer to pray.

4. We don't need to feel guilty about having a physical reaction around ovulation time. Women's bodies change week by week. Part of the normal and natural

monthly cycle involves having days when our body is more receptive to intercourse because that's the moment we are fertile. It's not a sin to experience physical changes, including a desire for sex, as the month goes on.

5. We don't need to feel guilty about being hurt. Sexual abuse, rape and harassment are sins committed against people. We do not need to carry the guilt of the sins of others. If you have been sinned against, God is not angry with you for what happened, and he is not angry with you for being wounded by it.

I've heard people express feelings of guilt for all these things, and the reality is that *there is nothing to be guilty about.* God does not want us to be the kind of people who scurry around and find extra things about which to feel bad! He is a loving Father, not a mean despot eager to make us cower.

Not just a feeling

When it comes to pornography, fantasy and erotica, however, there are some very tangible and serious ways in which we do rebel against God. It's not just that we feel bad, empty or alone when we do it; we indulge in direct disobedience. It's not merely that we *feel* guilty; it's that we *are* guilty. Rather than being faithful people who take seriously the command: "You shall have no other gods before me" (Exodus 20 v 3-5), when we pursue our idols, we mutiny against God in our hearts. That makes us profoundly guilty.

God is not like a manufacturer of vacuum cleaners. Manufacturers always include an instruction booklet with their product; some even include one that is vaguely coherent.

It's there to tell us how to get the best out of our appliance; to show what each of the attachments does and so on. And it's not a bad idea to read it. But I'm willing to state with a high degree of confidence that the managing directors of Samsung and Electrolux don't lie awake at night thinking about the fact that we used the curtain attachment to clean out the cat bed. They are keen to tell us how to use their appliance safely and optimally, but actually don't really care if we use it in some other way.

God cares. When we use our bodies and minds in ways that go against his revealed will in Scripture, God minds a great deal.

Broken mirrors

All humans are made in God's image. When other people look at us, they get a glimpse of what God is like. There are many ways in which we reflect his image, but two ways that are particularly relevant here are holiness and truth. Humans were designed to, and Christians are able to, show the world that God's ways are pure and God's priorities are correct. When we read erotic material, watch online sex or indulge in a fantasy world, we give the impression that purity doesn't matter and idols are just as good as the one true God.

It's sometimes easy to forget, but when God says that we shouldn't worship anyone or anything other than him, he isn't being a controlling despot or a petty functionary—he is merely giving an accurate statement about what is right and what is good for us. Pursuing other gods is just plain pointless. Elijah grasped that fact as well as any biblical character.

Elijah went head to head with the idols of his culture in a story recorded in 1 Kings 18. He was surrounded by Baal worshippers. Baal's followers believed their god promised a lot: rain, crops and fertility. And if you lived in a subsistence agricultural culture, those things mattered. When rain failed and crops faltered, many of the inhabitants of the land were quick to dump the one true God, withdraw from God's true community and turn to Baal instead.

Trouble is, Baal was a rubbish god. To put it bluntly, he couldn't even light a fire!

The 450 priests of Baal did their best; in fact, they went to extraordinary lengths to encourage their god to act.

They called on the name of Baal from morning till noon … they danced around … they shouted louder and slashed themselves with swords and spears … but there was no response, no one answered, no one paid attention. (1 Kings 18 v 26-29)

Their made-up god did absolutely nothing for them. Not even the tiniest, fleeting spark came from his hands.

Then Elijah poured water all over his altar, and simply prayed:

LORD, the God of Abraham, Isaac and Israel, let it be known today that you are God in Israel. (v 36)

What happened?

The fire of the LORD fell and burned up the sacrifice, the wood, the stones and the soil, and also licked up the water in the trench. (v 38)

There's just no comparison. Fake gods are pathetic; the real God is awesome.

When God says to avoid idols, he's doing it for his glory and our good. When he encourages us to trust him rather than pursue the idol of control, when he tells us to want him more than experience, he is telling us the right thing to do and trying to stop us doing something as utterly pointless as dancing around in a circle trying to get a block of stone to light a fire.

If we choose to ignore his words, we dump the great Ruler of the universe, replace him with a cheap substitute, and end up doing the most ridiculous things that cause us untold pain and separate us from the rest of God's community. We distance ourselves from our Maker, use our bodies and minds for impurity rather than purity, and put ourselves in a position where we deserve punishment.

Broken minds

When we create a fantasy world or watch pornography, we engage in sexual activity with other people without having a relationship with them.

Most of the time, when we watch porn, we have no idea what the real names of the actors and actresses are. We don't know where they grew up or what their favourite flavour of ice-cream is. We don't even know if they have chosen a life of adult film-making, whether they're earning money any way they can to feed a drug habit, or whether they are the victims of sex-traffickers who hold their passports and control their every move with threats of violence. We don't know, and we don't want to know, because knowing would involve seeing them as human beings, and that would get in the way of our idol of relationship or experience or control.

If we allowed them to have a personality or an opinion, they wouldn't fit into our fantasies so well. It's much simpler to hold them at arm's length and use them as objects that help us to feel better about ourselves. It's easier to pay our money and pretend that everything's fine, and ignore the pain and exploitation that many adult actresses experience.

The Old Testament prophet Amos brought God's word to people who looked to their own desires at the expense of those around them; and the words aren't comforting.

> *This is what the LORD says:*
> *"For three sins of Israel,*
> *even for four, I will not relent.*
> *They sell the innocent for silver,*
> *and the needy for a pair of sandals.*
> *They trample on the heads of the poor*
> *as on the dust of the ground*
> *and deny justice to the oppressed ...*
> *Now then, I will crush you." (Amos 2 v 6-7, 13)*

Of course, we may not use actors online; we may use people we know, in our heads. But when we fantasise about becoming intimate with people we know, we usher them into a world where they have no ability to say "no" to us. We stop caring about what they want and use their voice and their image to fuel what we want. It's stealing. We stop treating people like people and start treating them like objects.

And we are having an affair with them. Jesus said:

> *... anyone who looks at a woman lustfully has already*
> *committed adultery with her in his heart.*
>
> *(Matthew 5 v 28)*

There is no reason to think that looking at a man lustfully is any less serious.

Not only are we exploiting and stealing from others; we are robbing our future partners, too. Research suggests that porn use causes desensitisation in our body. We are used to non-stop ecstasy. The reality of irritatingly-timed coughs or sneezes, cold bedrooms, screaming children in neighbouring rooms, and husbands who simply aren't getting turned on by what we are offering seems singularly unerotic. It has been suggested that pornography addiction can even rewrite the pathways in the brain to such an extent that it becomes next to impossible to pleasure a real life partner without the involvement of pornographic imagery.

Fantasy and pornography use damage other people—people God cares deeply about. And, as Amos points out, that puts us in a place where we deserve punishment.

Broken relationship

Hurting ourselves and our fellow humans is serious enough, but the biggest problem with using fantasy, erotica and pornography is that they damage our relationship with God. All sin (and sin is simply any way in which we wander away from God's way of living) is ultimately against God.

King David knew a thing or two about sexual immorality. He went far beyond imagining or viewing things that weren't pure. He saw the beautiful Bathsheba, his mind lingered on her, he fetched her and he slept with her (you can read about it in 2 Samuel 11). But that wasn't the end of it: he got her pregnant, tried to cover his tracks by inviting her husband back from battle to sleep with her and, when that failed, he had her husband killed. It's not hard to see how he hurt a lot of people in that catalogue of awfulness. And yet, when he finally came to his senses and looked at what he had done, he said to God:

> *Against you, you only, have I sinned and done what is*
> *evil in your sight. (Psalm 51 v 4)*

On one level, they are words that can leave us scratching our heads. *Are you sure, David? Only God?! I can certainly think of a few ways you've ruined other people's lives!* But they capture an important fact: no matter how much we hurt ourselves or others, those things pale into insignificance when compared with our rebellion against God.

Imagining sex with people other than our husband—whether that's fuelled by the video, literature or imagination alone—is an affront against God. He doesn't sit in heaven thinking it's of no consequence; he doesn't dismiss it as a bit of a laugh, and he doesn't see it as harmless. He hates it, and he will judge it.

Ezekiel 16 is one of the most sobering chapters in the Bible. It's the story of a baby; abandoned, rescued, nurtured, loved, married and lavished with good things, but who chooses to wander away from her husband and seek power, experience, popularity and security in the arms of other men:

> *You trusted in your beauty and used your fame to*
> *become a prostitute. You lavished your favours on*
> *anyone who passed by and your beauty became his.*
> *(Ezekiel 16 v 15)*

It's a sordid tale. And the real shock lies in the fact that God says it's a picture of the way in which his people treat him:

> *You took some of your garments to make gaudy high*
> *places [high places were where idols were worshipped],*
> *where you carried on your prostitution. (v 16)*

We have been rescued, welcomed into God's family, loved and showered with good things; but all too often we choose to throw those things away and pursue idols instead. We have become spiritual prostitutes.

Does that term shock you? Offend you? God says it is the reality. Each click of porn, every fantasy designed to dump God and create a world where we are in control and able to use other people for our own personal gratification—that's an act of prostitution. Not stand-on-a-street-corner-in-a-short-skirt prostitution—no, it is worse than that. It is spiritual adultery, unfaithfulness to God. We cheat on our Maker, and that's huge.

The appropriate response from God? The end of the relationship. The end of his love, care, and gifts. An eternity without him, without anything good, reaping the consequences of our adultery. That's hell.

Sexual sin matters:

> *For of this you can be sure: no immoral, impure or*
> *greedy person—such a person is an idolater—has any*
> *inheritance in the kingdom of Christ and of God.*
> *Let no one deceive you with empty words, for because*
> *of such things God's wrath comes on those who are*
> *disobedient. (Ephesians 5 v 5-6)*

The sexual sins we commit while alone are not more serious than other sins like greed, or sexual sins we commit with others; but they are not less serious, whatever we may tell ourselves. They are acts worthy of God's righteous anger.

You and I are guilty. We may feel it, or we may not. But in the courtroom of heaven, as our cheated Maker looks at us from his judge's seat, the facts are the facts. We are guilty. We deserve only anger and separation from God.

It's sobering stuff. Scary in the extreme. But thankfully, it's not the end of the story...

6. Mercy

I'm not someone who cries easily, but I sobbed the night I first saw my idolatry in all its horror.

That evening, as I sat reflecting on just how much I had rebelled against God, used others and hurt myself, the floodgates opened. I was overwhelmed by the enormity of my sin. I had been listening to culture's call not to worry about what I was doing, and ignoring God's good design for my life. Realising that I was in a pit of guilt was devastating. It was an awful few hours.

I started to ask myself some desperate questions:

"Does God still love me?"
"Does he want me in his family?"
"Is there any hope?"
"Can I ever change?"

You see, I'm a hippo at heart. When I see my sin, I get knocked down. I stare in disbelief at how I have dishonoured the One who loves me the most, and it feels as if the world has ended. Left to my own devices, I could stay wallowing in the mud and the mire for months, if not years. My natural tendency is to want to repeatedly berate myself. If I'm not careful, my inner monologue spirals out of control: "You idiot, how could you have been so stupid? Haven't you messed up enough in your life already? Can't you ever get it right? Won't you ever learn? You pathetic, useless, worthless waste of space…"

Over the years, I've learned the hard way that being a hippo doesn't work any more than being a frog does. Frogs live in denial, hippos live in a pit of self-loathing, and neither of those places solves the problem of our sin.

Thankfully, God comes looking for hippos and frogs with a wonderful gift that changes everything.

How to cry well

Ezekiel isn't the only book of the Bible that describes our unfaithfulness to God as prostitution. Hosea does too, and here the story's happy ending is fleshed out in much more detail. The book of Hosea is the astonishing account of a prophet who is called by God to marry a woman he knew would be unfaithful. It's a heart-rending tale of betrayal as the woman leaves her husband and falls into the arms of other men. Her sin is devastatingly obvious. But the way God asks Hosea to respond is jaw-droppingly surprising.

Hosea had been betrayed horribly. His wife had trashed their marriage, treated him with contempt, stamped on God's law and left him for another. God's instruction?

> *Go, show your love to your wife again, though she is loved by another man and is an adulteress. Love her as the LORD loves the Israelites, though they turn to other gods. (Hosea 3 v 1)*

Hosea was to be the kind of husband who went after his wayward spouse, continued loving her against the odds, and invited her back to live with him again—forgiven, restored and adored. Why?

Because that's exactly how God treats those who have pursued idols instead of him. We wander off. We use our minds and our bodies in all kinds of ways that are dishonouring. We follow our own desires, our own priorities. But that doesn't put God off. He doesn't dump us. He doesn't issue us with the divorce papers we deserve. He is so committed to us that he calls us back, brings us back, and urges us back to a life of faithfulness. He calls us to dump the things in our life that are fake and vile, and instead return to the privileged and fulfilled life, where he is put first.

The question is: *Will we make that change or not?*

Sometimes, crying at our own disobedience is a good thing to do. When Peter denied knowing Jesus, "he broke down and wept" (Mark 14 v 72). But Hosea shows that there are two ways to cry, two options when we are confronted by our sin, only one of which results in the reconciliation that God so clearly wants and we so desperately need. Not all tears are like Peter's. God said that the people in Hosea's day:

> … *do not cry out to me from their hearts but wail on their beds. (Hosea 7 v 14)*

Option One is to "wail on our beds". We've all been there. It's that moment when we feel awful and just want to let it all out. We tell our pillow all about it and we beat ourselves up for being such an idiot. But then we leave it at that. Those tears show that we regret things being the way they are, but leave us stagnant.

Judas was an Option One guy. After Jesus' death he was appalled at himself, and loathed what he had done. He found his actions so abhorrent that he took the unusually extreme step of taking his own life. He showed regret—but he showed it in a way that kept him enveloped in sin and heading towards judgment.

Crying on our beds can bring huge emotional release, but as the tears subside, all we're left with are puffy eyes, smudged mascara and damp duvets. Nothing of substance has actually changed. You can't cry guilt away. You need to give it away.

Option Two is to "cry out to God from our hearts". When we see our idolatry, our actions and our guilt, we can pour out our thoughts and feelings to the Lord who knows all things, hears all things and has the power to change all things. God is holy and he is huge but he is intimately involved in our lives and loves to hear us speak. There are few words he loves to hear more than a heart-felt: "I'm sorry". Like the perfect Father he is, he embraces those who return to him and admit they're in a mess and need his help. He forgives. And he acts in us to help us change.

It can feel hard to cry out to God. Any one of us who have been trapped in a fantasy world or addicted to pornography may be able to relate to that instinct to hide from God because the offer of mercy just doesn't seem credible. Sinners have been hiding from God since the first sin, when the first woman and her husband:

> *… heard the sound of the LORD God as he was walking in the garden in the cool of the day, and they hid from the LORD God among the trees of the garden.*
>
> *(Genesis 3 v 8)*

The further we wander from God, the more we feel we need to hide. If we've been involved in any of the extremes of pornography, that feeling can be especially powerful. The horrors of bestiality, rape scenarios or child abuse go beyond what even the most liberal in our society consider to be acceptable. Such clips are wrong—criminal, in fact—and surely God can't want to hear from people like that? Surely there is no way back from there? But he does and there is...

The prostitute's husband

The loving husband of Hosea 3 isn't just a chocolate-box picture of an abstract God; it's a concrete foretaste of Christ's saving work.

Hosea had every right to sit at home feeling angry. He had every right to rip into his wife, Gomer, for her appalling behaviour. He had every right to offer only a trial reunion, to see if she'd really changed.

He did none of those things.

> *I bought her for fifteens shekels of silver and about a homer and a lethek of barley. Then I told her, "You are to live with me for many days; you must not be a prostitute or be intimate with any man, and I will behave the same way toward you." (Hosea 3 v 2-3)*

Hosea pursued his wife. He poured out his love. He paid what he needed to free her from her "lover". He committed himself to her, long term. He called her to live in a relationship with him that would see her loved, secure, fulfilled.

This really happened. And it is truly astonishing. Can you imagine how Gomer must have felt? A man she had hurt so badly and betrayed so deeply was willing to set aside his status, his rights, and his wealth, and welcome her back into his home for the rest of her life. Wow!

You and I are Gomer. And our Hosea is the Lord Jesus, God the Son. He came for us.

The Son of Man did not come to be served, but to serve, and to give his life as a ransom for many.

(Mark 10 v 45)

When he hung on his cross, in physical agony and spiritual isolation, he lovingly took the sins of rebellious people upon himself. He paid the price of our spiritual adultery, and he did it completely. Your use of pornography. The things you've read. The fantasies you've created. Jesus dealt with it on the cross. He paid the price. He came for you.

There is no sin so deep or so miserable that Jesus didn't pay for it. When he rose from the dead three days later, he didn't say: *Oops—I forgot about pornography and fantasy.* He didn't say: *Sorry, but pornography and fantasy are just too impure for me to want to die for.* He dealt with it. In Jesus there *is* forgiveness. There is forgiveness for me; there is forgiveness for you. There is no sin we do not need him to die for; there is no sin he has not died for. No matter how low we have sunk, God's mercy is wide enough, deep enough and wonderful enough to reach us.

If you are not yet a Christian, this mercy, this forgiveness is on offer to you. Will you come to him, admit your sin and its seriousness, and give your guilt to him? Will you let him carry it to the cross, pay the price to free you from it, and hear him say: *I have dealt with it.*

If you are a Christian already, remember afresh just how wonderful your Saviour is. Hear him say to you:

I've taken the punishment, paid the penalty, washed you clean Yes, you have sinned again, and again—but my blood has covered it all. Now live in faithfulness with me. Enjoy your relationship with me. I love you.

Forgiven past

Whether you have been a Christian for 30 years or 30 seconds, are you ready to say sorry for the fantasy, erotica and pornography you've engaged in? Every adulterous thought that has passed through your mind's eye, every click on the shortcut to porn, every literature-fuelled foray into sexual immorality… are you willing to lay them before God? All we have to do is be real about our sin and ask for God's forgiveness through Jesus.

Denying we have a problem won't work. Seeking restoration by trying to be extra good in other areas of our life is utterly futile. Finding forgiveness for past sins—whether they are related to sex or any other form of rebellion against God—is about honesty and humility before the Lord. As the apostle John reminds us:

If we claim to be without sin, we deceive ourselves and the truth is not in us. If we confess our sins, he is faithful and just and will forgive us our sins and purify us from all unrighteousness. (1 John 1 v 8-9)

There's no set place to ask for forgiveness—in the bath is just as good as in church. There's no set position to assume—on my knees tends to work for me, but if you're reading this on a bus, I suggest you stay in your seat. There are no set words we have to utter—any prayer that says sorry, asks for forgiveness and seeks help to live differently is a delight to God. But you can't do much better than Psalm 51, that psalm written by King David when he was confronted by his sexually wayward past. It has been used by many Christians since as a framework for returning to the Lord.

Why not read the words slowly, reflectively, personally. Be specific about the things you are sorry for, and the ways in which you want to change both in your attitudes and your actions.

Have mercy on me, O God,
according to your unfailing love;
according to your great compassion
blot out my transgressions.
Wash away all my iniquity
and cleanse me from my sin.

For I know my transgressions,
and my sin is always before me.
Against you, you only, have I sinned
and done what is evil in your sight;
so you are right in your verdict
and justified when you judge.
Surely I was sinful at birth,
sinful from the time my mother conceived me.
Yet you desired faithfulness even in the womb;
you taught me wisdom in that secret place.

Cleanse me with hyssop, and I shall be clean;
wash me, and I shall be whiter than snow.
Let me hear joy and gladness;

let the bones you have crushed rejoice.
Hide your face from my sins
and blot out all my iniquity.

Create in me a pure heart, O God,
and renew a steadfast spirit within me.
Do not cast me from your presence
or take your Holy Spirit from me.
Restore to me the joy of your salvation
and grant me a willing spirit, to sustain me.

Then I will teach transgressors your ways,
so that sinners will turn back to you.
Deliver me from the guilt of bloodshed, O God,
you who are God my Saviour,
and my tongue will sing of your righteousness.
Open my lips, Lord,
and my mouth will declare your praise.
You do not delight in sacrifice, or I would bring it;
you do not take pleasure in burnt offerings.
My sacrifice, O God, is a broken spirit;
a broken and contrite heart
you, God, will not despise.

May it please you to prosper Zion,
to build up the walls of Jerusalem.
Then you will delight in the sacrifices of the righteous,
in burnt offerings offered whole;
then bulls will be offered on your altar.

We don't get a lot of snow where I live in London; and when it does fall, it gets pretty slushy very quickly. But most of us have at some stage experienced just how lovely freshly fallen, deep snow is. It's so white that it almost radiates light. It looks so pure, so clean, so beautiful.

When people are washed by God, they are "whiter than snow".

Do you know that Jesus died for you? Then you are even cleaner, purer and more beautiful than fresh snow. Yes, really, that's you.

Feeling reality

"But I don't feel it!" you may protest. "I still feel tainted. Just look at my past. How can I not?!"

Feelings can be wonderful, but they can also be desperately deceptive. Remember, it was feeling we needed something more than what God wants for us that got us into this mess in the first place. And, if we're not careful, it is feelings that can keep us from believing that God has truly dealt with our sin. God's acceptance of you doesn't depend on how you feel—it depends on the facts of Jesus' death and resurrection. So facts are what we need to focus on. And, through Christ, the fact is that, if we have admitted our sin and asked for forgiveness, we are truly, perfectly clean. Fact.

It may take some time to get to grips with this. We all need to challenge our miserable feelings with the wonderful facts, and discipline ourselves not to let our wayward feelings cause us to disbelieve the truth. At times, I have had to remind myself of the wonders of God's generosity every hour, every day. But when the truth sinks in, it's the best feeling ever, because it's the most exciting gift a human being can receive!

The sin and stains that have marred our lives in the past

have been passed to Christ. The beauty and purity that are his by nature have been passed to us, despite our behaviour. God has clothed us with righteousness. Our old life has been completely washed away and we've been covered by Jesus' purity. Astonishing.

Forgiven future

I'd like to be able to tell you that once I had repented, I never did anything sexually immoral ever again. I would so love to be able to tell you that. It would be a fairly-tale ending, wouldn't it: *Girl caught in web of sexual intrigue turns to Jesus and joyfully embraces purity every moment for the rest of her life...*

My life is no fairy tale.

There are some people who repent of a particular sin and then, in God's goodness, never go near it again. And praise the Lord for his work in those people! But, for many of us, the route to change is a long, slow slog. There will be days when we revel in our new-found beauty and live in a beautiful purity that matches our status before God. There will be other days when we sink back into fantasy and pornography: maybe for a few moments, maybe for longer. We may struggle with this for years—for the rest of our life here on earth.

I hope that doesn't discourage you. I simply want to be honest about what life is like. You will sin. The great news is that the power of the cross covers future sins too.

Christ's death covers *all* sins—including those we haven't committed yet. This is one of the things we need to hear most in life. Just like Hosea with his wife, no matter how many times we mess up, God is aching to see us turn back to a life of faithfulness.

God is patient with us long after we become exasperated with ourselves. He is working to change us even when the evidence seems to suggest we're beyond hope. His grace—his willingness to shower good things on us when we don't deserve any of them—is unending.

For those of us who find ourselves repeatedly messing up again and again, James 4 v 6 is a precious verse. James is writing to Christians, but he calls them "adulterous people". How striking—he applies Ezekiel and Hosea's language to Christians. These Christians are like us. They love Jesus, but they keep on cheating on him by loving things in the world more. It's why James 4 v 6 is so wonderful:

But he gives us more grace.

More grace. Each time we mess up, God remembers the cross and pours more forgiveness into our lives. Each time we act like an adulterous wife, God remembers that the cross does what is necessary to enable us to return to a life of faithfulness. If we are following Jesus, our sin will never, can never, outweigh his mercy.

He is that generous.

There is always more grace.

This doesn't mean we can use our forgiveness as an excuse to enter our online or fantasy world again with a license for lust. It's not unknown for people to say: "Well, if God has forgiven me anyway, I might as well just indulge". But James continues:

God opposes the proud but shows favour to the humble.

(v 6)

Pride says: *God will forgive me, so I'll keep living how I like.*

Humility says: *God has forgiven my sin, so I want to live how he likes.*

Knowing we're forgiven sinners is supposed to spur us on to living life God's way, not to further rebellion. Being forgiven of adultery is something that's designed to encourage us to pursue purity with ever-increasing passion.

So if and when, despite prayer and hard work, the stumble comes, we don't need to doubt our status as precious members of God's family. We don't need to doubt his love. And we don't need to doubt our forgiveness. All those things are rock-solid facts. We simply need to acknowledge that we've been disobedient, ask for his forgiveness, and seek his help to keep changing our hearts and behaviour. Just like Gomer in Hosea 3, once we change direction, we can settle into a life of restored relationship and renewed commitment to God, safe in the knowledge that he is not going anywhere.

Forgiven present

With our past dealt with and our future secure, we're able to focus on what being forgiven means for us in the present. How does knowing we are treasured, adored, cleaned children of God impact us today?

Queen Elizabeth II's mother is reputed to have told Princess Elizabeth and her sister, Margaret, when they were young: "Royal children must display royal manners". She was keen to emphasise that being royalty was about more than having a title—the title needs living up to. Their good behaviour did not secure their status; their bad behaviour did not threaten their royalty. But their status should motivate a standard of behaviour that matched it.

We are royal children, not of some British monarch, but of the King of the Universe. And royal children should display royal manners. How do we live as part of this eternal royal family? How do we show who our Father is, and how wonderful he is? That's where we turn, as forgiven children, in our next two chapters.

7. Purity

When I first wanted to break free from my own inner fantasy world, I had quite a naïve view of what the process of transformation would be like. I thought that all I had to do was remember that God loves me, pray for his help and then everything would be alright. Of course, it wasn't! Thankfully, the Bible is not that naïve about how people change.

In his letter to the church in Ephesus, Paul uses a great metaphor:

> *You were taught, with regard to your former way of life, to put off your old self, which is being corrupted by its deceitful desires ... and to put on the new self, created to be like God in true righteousness and holiness.*
> *(Ephesians 4 v 22, 24)*

The Christian life—breaking free from destructive, sinful habits and becoming more like Jesus—is like changing our clothes. There are things we need to take off, and other things we need to put on.

Pond day

When I was a child, we had a pond in our garden. It was home to goldfish, newts, frogs and, most notably, epic quantities of sludge. Once a year came "pond day" when, armed with fishing nets, buckets and brushes, my mother and I would catch the things that lived and scrub the things that oozed. It was a smelly, wriggly day.

The worst part of pond day was removing the near-stagnant water at the base of the pond—it stank. I have never quite grasped why but every year, without fail, I managed to pour a bucket of the stuff over myself. Sooner or later, a moment's lapse in concentration would result in a rancid mass of green and brown gloop oozing down my t-shirt, turning me into a festering popsicle of grime. After a withering look and a few expressions of despair, my mother would give me detailed instructions on where to put my slimy garments and where to find cleaner replacements. I desperately needed a change of clothes.

Moving from a life of fantasy or pornography to a life of freedom and beauty is not so different. We cannot put on clean clothes until we remove our dirty ones.

What clothes to take off

The first thing we need to take off is our idolatry—the "deceitful desires" (Ephesians 4 v 22) of our hearts. We need to get rid of the things we want more than God.

That doesn't mean dumping all desires. We're not called to a Buddhist path of seeing desire as unhelpful. We're not called to take refuge in the nearest convent to develop poverty, chastity and obedience in solitude. The Bible has no problem with desire:

> *As the deer pants for streams of water, so my soul pants*
> *for you, my God. (Psalm 42 v 1)*

> *We groan, longing to be clothed ... with our heavenly*
> *dwelling. (2 Corinthians 5 v 2)*

Desires, when well directed, are great!

But our "over-desires" (as Ephesians 4 v 22 could be helpfully translated) are destructive. When we desire things more than we desire God—when we pant for something more than we pant for knowing Christ—we're over-desiring the wrong things.

And we need to get rid of these idols with as much passion as an Old Testament king called Josiah.

When Josiah was in his twenties, he ordered some repairs to be done on the temple. His father and grandfather had tolerated and sometimes even promoted idolatry, and the country was in a terrible state as a result. Shrines and altars to false gods were everywhere, the temple where God dwelled among his people was neglected, and people's lifestyles were spiralling away from the Lord.

In the course of the temple work, the "book of the law" (probably Deuteronomy) was rediscovered and read to the king. Josiah was cut to the quick. The words left him in no doubt that God was angry with the idolatry in the land.

Josiah was neither a hippo nor a frog. He repented and recommitted himself and his people to God. He shared what he had learned and then set about a programme of destruction:

> *He took the Asherah pole from the temple of the LORD*
> *to the Kidron Valley outside Jerusalem and burned it*
> *there. He ground it to powder and scattered the dust*
> *over the graves of the common people. He also tore down*

> *the quarters of the male shrine-prostitutes that were in*
> *the temple of the LORD, the quarters where women did*
> *weaving for Asherah. (2 Kings 23 v 6-8)*

Notice what he did with his idols. He took them down. He burned them. He ground them to powder.

Our call is to do the same.

Of course, wooden poles and stone statues are easier to smash than inner idols. We can't just reach into our hearts, grab the bit that contains our wayward hopes and dreams, and destroy it. But we can follow Josiah's lead and work through the process of allowing Scripture to reveal our idols; being grieved by our idols; and choosing to live without our idols.

Taking off idols by seeing idols

Reading the Bible improves our vision. As we see the holiness of God in the pages of his word, and compare ourselves to the Bible's teaching on what it is to be a child of God, we begin to see ourselves more clearly. We see our idols.

Hopefully, reading this book will have started that process, but I'm only human and my book is fallible. God's book is perfect. Regular engagement with his living and active word is the only real way to see, and keep seeing, the areas in which we need to change.

I used to think I hadn't committed adultery. I can say, honestly, I have never slept with or kissed a married man. But then I read the Sermon on the Mount:

> *Anyone who looks at a woman lustfully has already*
> *committed adultery with her in his heart.*
>
> *(Matthew 5 v 28)*

I have looked at people lustfully. I have wanted sex with someone I'm not married to. I have fantasised about doing that. I have wanted someone more than I have wanted faithfulness to God; and that's adultery. I would never have worked that out on my own. I needed the Bible to show me that truth.

"Be[ing] made new in the attitude of your minds" (Ephesians 4 v 23) isn't a one-off event. It's a lifestyle, a continual drive to see our idols more clearly. And so step one of putting off our idols is to be passionate about engaging with Scripture. Not in a routine "I'm going to skim-read a psalm" kind of way. No, we need to approach the Bible saying: "Lord, I want to be more in love with you, and be more like you; and I need you to show me the areas of my life that need to change". That's how we begin to see our idols, so that we can begin to take them off.

Taking off idols by hating idols

Once we see our idols, we need to hate them. Not just hate what they encourage us to do—the fantasy or the pornography—but hate them for what they are: stumbling blocks in our relationship with God. An idol is something you are, spiritually speaking, cheating on God with.

Hate is a strong emotion and not one usually encouraged in godly women, but it's entirely appropriate in this context. When Josiah saw the idols in his territory, he was grieved: he tore his clothes, he wept and he razed the idols to the ground. Not exactly a mild reaction! He expressed strong emotions because idols are so dangerous.

For as long as we see our idols as mild, innocuous or merely unfortunate, we will never long to get rid of them.

I have a place on my forehead where a pimple keeps popping up. I call it my white chocolate pimple because it always seems to appear just after I've overdone the Lindt treats. When I see the spot, I sigh slightly. I wish it weren't there but I don't feel strongly about it. Last year, when I found a lump in my breast, I was not so calm. Ignoring it didn't even cross my mind. I was straight off to the doctors to do whatever was needed to get rid of it. I hated the thought of that lump being there. I wanted it gone.

Have you seen that your idols are dangerous lumps, not pimples? If you are to rid yourself of them, you have to want them out. You need to learn to hate those desires; to learn to hate anything in your heart that gets in the way of your relationship with Jesus.

Do you want your idols out with the passion they deserve?

Taking off idols by choosing to live without idols

Josiah didn't just gently dismantle the idols in his land and store them somewhere safe, in case they might come in handy at a later date. He had the idols ground to dust. Why? Because he wanted to ensure they could never be worshipped again. He made a choice, a choice that said: "Idols are off limits in my land".

We need to make a choice too. We have no land to lead; we do have a life. We need to get to the point where we can say: "OK, Lord, I've had enough. I'm fed up of this idol controlling my life. I want you to be in charge. I want my security to be in you. I want my fulfilment to be found in you. I choose to live without this idol. Please change me."

If you can't say that right now, you can always go back a step.

You can ask God to help you want to live without your idols. But sooner or later, if you are to change, you have to choose to live wholeheartedly, not half-heartedly, for Christ. That can feel a bit scary if your fantasy or your pornography has been a regular companion and a source of comfort for many years. But Christ is a better friend, and he is where true comfort can be found. Choosing to grind up your idol is a hard choice, but it's a great one, and one you will never regret.

Taking off impure thoughts

When I first got my cat, Molly, she was not a cute and cuddly creature. In fact, a vet told me it would probably be best to have her put down because she was so out of control following the abuse she had experienced. So I knew I was in for a rough ride! To be honest, she wasn't so much a feline as a whirring mass of teeth and claws, loosely held together by some black fur. It took 12 months of consistent, gentle discipline and love—and a lot of bandages—but eventually she was tamed.

Sometimes my brain seems as out of control as a wild cat. Thoughts pop into my mind from nowhere. Maybe you know that feeling too. You don't want to think about sexually immoral material, but it just seems to appear. The good news is that, in the power of the Spirit, our minds can be tamed too.

We do this by doing two things, with the Spirit's help.

Taking off impure thoughts by running away

When Joseph was working as a slave in Potiphar's house, he found himself in a compromising situation. His boss's wife made a pass at him. How did he respond? He "ran out of the house" (Genesis 39 v 12). He didn't want to get into a sexually improper situation, and so he ran. He did what Paul would tell the Corinthian church to do: "Flee from sexual immorality" (1 Corinthians 6 v 18).

We can do that in our minds too. Whenever we feel a fantasy coming on, we can have a quiet word: "Seriously? You want to go down that route again? You want to let your idol win? You want to turn your back on God? Come on, run away. Run away now. Think about something else." Talking to yourself is not a sign of madness—it is the path to godliness! It's liberating to be able to tell ourselves: "No".

And, of course, we can run away from things that are likely to trigger fantasy or pornography use. We can run away or stay away from films that are unhelpfully suggestive or explicit; we can run away from TV programmes that are likely to give us images to replay; we can run away from books that contain erotic scenes (by not buying them, or throwing them away, and asking friends to keep us accountable); we can change our route to work if there is a specific person who is catching our eye.

You can put verses like 1 Corinthians 6 v 18 in the places where you know you struggle—maybe on your phone's lockscreen, in your bedroom or at your desk. And you can ask close friends to text you reminders too. There is no shame in running away. Running away from idols means you are running towards purity.

Taking off impure thoughts by fighting back

Sometimes, though, it's good to stand our ground against wayward thinking. That's what Jesus did when he was tempted by the devil in the desert. Satan offered him food, power and safety—hugely tempting for someone who was hungry and knew that his life was leading him to a cross. How did Jesus react? He quoted Scripture. He used the most powerful weapon there is in the war against temptation; what Paul called the "sword of the Spirit" (Ephesians 6 v 17).

Three times the devil tempts Jesus. Three times Jesus stands his ground, each answer starting: "It is written" or "It is said" (Luke 4 v 1-13). When temptation hits, when evil crouches at our door, we can dispatch it with words of truth. When we want to run to fantasy-land for security at the end of a stressful day, we can say:

> It is written… *The LORD is my strength and my shield.*
> *(Psalm 28 v 7)*

When it feels as if porn is the only antidote to the deep, depressing isolation we are experiencing, we can say:

> It is written… *See what great love the Father has*
> *lavished on us, that we should be called children of God!*
> *And that is what we are! (1 John 3 v 1)*

You know your idol—you can get your armoury of verses ready!

Of course, fighting the thoughts that say: "You're never going to kick this habit" or: "You'll give in eventually, so why not just do it now?" or: "God doesn't love you enough to change you really" is just as important as fighting the sexually impure thoughts. Again, Scripture is your weapon:

> *God is faithful; he will not let you be tempted beyond*
> *what you can bear. But when you are tempted, he will*
> *also provide a way out so that you can endure it.*
> *(1 Corinthians 10 v 13)*

> *[Nothing] ... in all creation will be able to separate us*
> *from the love of God that is in Christ Jesus our Lord.*
> *(Romans 8 v 39)*

Anything that's a lie needs slapping down with truth.

We need to be wise to the devil's tactics and ready to defend ourselves. Ask yourself the question: "If I were Satan, what tactics would I use to trip me up?" If you can identify your vulnerabilities and name the strategies that Satan has in his toolbox, you can shame him, expose him and be better equipped to defeat him. And we need to have Scripture at our fingertips. If you're struggling to think of suitable verses, why not meet up with a mature Christian from church? I'll bet they'd love to help you identify truths that will set you free.

Taking off impure actions

Worshipping idols leads to impure thoughts... and impure thoughts lead to impure actions. So, if we take off our idols and our sexually inappropriate thoughts, we will probably find our actions start to change quite naturally. But putting some practical strategies in place can be a great help too.

Jesus, in his Sermon on the Mount, painted a vivid word-picture of the kind of lengths he wants his children to go to, to avoid sin:

> *And if your right hand causes you to stumble, cut it off*
> *and throw it away. It is better for you to lose one part of*
> *your body than for your whole body to go into hell.*
> *(Matthew 5 v 30)*

Jesus was not advocating a theology of holiness by amputation! It's an image. But what he was advocating is in a sense no less challenging; be ruthlessly radical and utterly wholehearted in your battle against sin.

What does that mean for us? Well, it's going to look very different for each of us, but here are some ideas…

1. If temptation hits during the day, try to make sure you're not alone. You won't watch porn if you're in an adult-education class or in a craft café with your kids, so get out of the house.

2. Dump your fantasy partners, and spend more time with real people. Be intentional about meeting up with people with whom you can give and receive encouragement.

3. Aim to release your endorphins without sexual arousal. Sport is a great option.

4. Get rid of any sex toys you may have amassed for use during fantasy or pornography.

5. Cancel any subscriptions to explicit material—paper or electronic.

6. Make yourself accountable for your internet use. The subscription to a service like Covenant Eyes (covenanteyes.com) is well worth it—using it will mean nominated friends will get to see exactly which dodgy sites you have visited, which is quite a deterrent!

7. And if all else fails, get rid of your TV and your computer… even your phone, at least for a while. A technology fast can be liberating. And it's better to miss out on all the good things technology offers you than to miss out on purity.

The options are endless. The key is to find and then enact what works for you—and to do so consistently, passionately and wholeheartedly.

You will not find this easy. One thing I learned on "pond day" was that dirty, slimy clothes don't come off easily. They cling. I had quite literally to wrestle the garments off my being and, on more than one occasion, wobbled in the struggle. But they did come off.

The strategies we've been looking at here won't necessarily stop every slip back into sexual immorality. The Christian life is one of constant repentance and forgiveness. But they will help. And by deliberately taking off the things that ensnare you, you can begin to break free. Step by step (including some backwards ones), you will begin to walk towards a life of beautiful purity. It's not a vague, elusive, out-of-reach hope— it's a real path of change.

Of course, changing clothes doesn't stop there. Change involves putting on as well as taking off. And as God's children, we have an exciting wardrobe of garments to put on in place of our filthy rags.

8. Liberty

Here's one of my best-kept secrets (until now): when I was in my teens, I was seriously into the band *Transvision Vamp*. I couldn't even begin to imagine walking along the street without having *Baby I don't care* blaring out of my Sony Walkman. The words resonated with my teenage angst; the music gave life to my innermost thoughts.

And soon I began to dress like the band around which my identity centred. Hefty black boots, enormous pieces of jewellery, lacy tops and excessive quantities of black eye-liner were my accessories of choice. I needed to express myself through what I wore. I needed to show the world who I truly was.

After a while, my taste in music mellowed. The band's lyrics no longer effectively expressed what I was thinking and feeling. I ceased to find my identity in alternative rock. And, as I changed on the inside, so my clothes changed on the outside. I wore outfits that were softer, gentler and less likely to give my parents heart failure.

When we become Christians, we are given a whole new identity. We are no longer rebels at war with the King of the universe—instead, we become his "dearly loved children" (Ephesians 5 v 1). And we are children with a royal commission. So now we gradually take off the clothes that rebels wear and instead put on the clothes that royal children wear. What are those new clothes? Well, in a sense the question is really: *Who* are those new clothes?

> *Clothe yourselves with the Lord Jesus Christ, and do not think about how to gratify the desires of the flesh.*
> *(Romans 13 v 14)*

Jesus is what we wear. The Christian life (as we saw way back in Chapter Two) is about becoming more beautiful, more pure… more and more like Jesus, our royal brother.

The problem is that putting on these new clothes doesn't come easily to most of us! That's partly because we struggle to understand our new identity, and partly because we struggle to think and act in accordance with our new identity.

Many of us go through our Christian lives able to come out with great doctrinal soundbites, but without actually letting the truth of them sink in. We praise God for "cleansing us by the blood of the Lamb", and then go home feeling guilty. We thank God for being "sovereign and good", and then do a headless-chicken routine because the world feels so out of control. We talk of our Lord's "unfailing love", and then mope about, wallowing in how alone and shunned we feel. We encourage others to run to God as their "rock and refuge", and then, when tough times hit, run in exactly the opposite direction and head straight for the trashy TV or the porn shortcut to bring us the comfort we so desperately need.

We only half get our faith. And so we only half change.

Time and time again we take off our old clothes of fantasy, erotica and pornography (because we see how important that is). And then a few days or weeks later, feeling exposed, we run back to the recycling bin, pull out our rags and put our filthy clothes back on. We rarely get as far as putting on our new clothes.

New identity

When was the last time you let the truths about your identity sink in? When was the last time you simply sat and thanked God for all the blessings that come from being "in Christ"? How good are you at catching yourself and correcting yourself when you think and say things that are contrary to your true identity?

Elephants never forget, the old saying goes. But I am no elephant: on an almost daily basis I forget how much God loves me, and what a privilege it is to be surrounded by brothers and sisters in Christ who are helping me become more like Jesus. I don't have a spiritual memory so much as a spiritual forget-ory, where gospel truths drip relentlessly out of my being. Which is why it is so important to remind myself of who I am.

Ephesians 1 is a goldmine of gospel truths that flesh out what it means for us to be God's adored children. When we are "in Christ", we share Jesus' relationship with the Father and that makes us astonishingly fortunate. Let's dip into just some of the verses:

1. "Praise be to the God and Father of our Lord Jesus Christ, who has blessed us in the heavenly realms with every spiritual blessing in Christ" (v 3). If you are

God's child, then you are privileged beyond measure, spiritually rich beyond your wildest imaginings! Your heavenly Father doesn't hold back. You have been and still are being showered with love, grace and mercy; and you have the best future possible to look forward to.

2. "For he chose us in him before the creation of the world to be holy and blameless in his sight" (v 4). That's how long you have been on God's mind, and that's how much he wants you to pursue purity. You might have known God for a few years or decades; but he has known you for millennia! You might have been pondering the matter of purity for a few hours or months, but he has been planning for you to journey towards Christ-likeness before you were even a twinkle in your great, great, great-grandparents' (or, indeed, Adam and Eve's) eyes!

3. "In love he predestined us for adoption to sonship through Jesus Christ, in accordance with his pleasure and will" (v 4-5). How amazing to be hand-picked to join God's family. And how amazing that he's happy to have us around. This is no reluctant uncle that tolerates his extended family only on high days and holidays—no, God is pleased—genuinely thrilled—to have you close to him.

4. "... to the praise of his glorious grace, which he has freely given us in the One he loves" (v 6). You don't deserve it, you haven't earned it; you certainly could never buy it, but he has given you forgiveness in abundance anyway. Your sins are gone. You are washed clean. There is not a hint of impurity messing up your relationship with

God anymore. You are a precious child in wonderful relationship with your precious Father.

5. "In him we have redemption through his blood, the forgiveness of sins, in accordance with the riches of God's grace" (v 7). You've been bought back at the cost of Jesus' very life, and are back in the arms of your gentle, loving Father, from where you can never be lost. It cost Jesus everything to save us; but that was a price he was willing to pay. What a brother he is!

6. "You were marked in him with a seal, the promised Holy Spirit, who is a deposit guaranteeing our inheritance until the redemption of those who are God's possession—to the praise of his glory" (v 13-14). God is at home in you and will be with you for ever. You are secure and headed for perfection, along with countless sisters and brothers. In Christ, there is no such thing as an unhappy ending. With our Father in charge, it's all going to be great in the end.

We are *so* privileged! *So* blessed! *So* overwhelmingly adored and provided for. *So* thoroughly called to a life characterised by purity. It's mind-blowing!

There's no room in these verses for: *But I'm too messed up* or: *Surely I've failed once too many times.* There are no exceptions for people who feel: *But that can't include me* or: *I'm not really cut out for this holiness thing* or: *I'm too old to change.* If you are following Jesus, then this is you. Eternally you. This is who God has declared you to be, and decreed you will become. And by his Spirit, he has made it completely possible.

Our challenge as Christians is to remember these facts, to enjoy these truths, and to let them seep into every part of our being. And we can help each other to keep holding on to them by texting, emailing, facebooking, tweeting, and speaking these things out—loud and clear—to our sisters in Christ, so we can never forget or doubt what God has said.

When we really get our identity—when we truly see ourselves as God sees us (as much as we can this side of heaven)—then it will become ever more natural to think and act in different ways.

Perhaps it is worth putting this book down for a little while, reading Ephesians 1, and thanking God for how he sees you right this moment, asking him to help you see yourself in that way too.

New minds

People with new identities think new thoughts. And, as we grow in our Christian lives, we think thoughts that are increasingly like Christ's.

There is a school of thought that encourages Christians to "let go and let God"; that assumes God will do all this work of change. We just sit round, revelling in the love that he has lavished upon us, and expect to wake up every morning a wiser and purer person.

It's true that the work of change is God's; but the apostle Paul saw that we have to put in some hard yards too. He says that Christians are "taught ... to be made new in the attitude of [our] minds" (Ephesians 4 v 23). Thinking new thoughts is something we actively need to learn how to do.

Have you ever tried to learn a new language? It's no easy task. Some years ago, I thought I'd have a go at learning Hebrew. It was great fun, but such hard work. For the first two weeks, I had the Hebrew alphabet song playing on a loop on my MP4. Each morning, it was vocabulary flashcards before work. Each evening, I practised writing from right to left. I threw myself into the work with absolute dedication but still, after a few months, I could translate little more than "the bread is on the table". Hardly the stuff of linguistic accomplishment.

Developing a new mind is like learning to think a new language. It's not a completely unfamiliar language—it's learning to think as we were designed to think in the first place. And it's not a process we have to undertake alone— the Holy Spirit is helping us every step of the way. But it does involve radical change and a not inconsiderable amount of effort on our part.

It's worth it, though—it will result in exciting change. The heart that has dumped the idol of control has a massive opportunity to grow in trust. The heart that has ditched the idol of experience has the chance to foster true contentment. The heart that has dropped the idol of relationships has the privilege of becoming ever more intimate with the One who loves the best. And we do all that by meeting God in his word and acting on what we find there.

Each time we read God's word alone... each time we meet with a friend to discuss what we have been reading in Scripture... each time we go to a Bible study... each time we hear a sermon or conference talk... we are being exposed to truth. If we choose to accept it, our mind gets a little more renewed.

In the longest psalm, the songwriter poses the question:

How can a young person stay on the path of purity?
(Psalm 119 v 9)

The answer?

By living according to your word.

We learn to trust God when we see in his word how trustworthy he is and we work to apply that to the circumstances we face day by day. We learn to become content when we believe the Bible's promise that God has given us everything we need. We learn to relate better to one another when we believe what God's word says his design for relationships is. We learn to be holy when we see in the Scriptures how immeasurably more beautiful it is to be walking with the Lord than it is to be pulling away from his loving hand like a petulant child.

Of course, we can only do this with God's help. And we need to ask for it—whoever we are. Have you ever noticed how much time Jesus spent quietly praying? In his three-year ministry, he travelled widely, spoke to hordes and healed hundreds. He was so well known in that corner of the world that he couldn't even go to visit his mother without it becoming a major gathering. And all the while, he was on a mission to save the world—as workloads go, it doesn't get more pressing than that! Added to all that, he was the perfect Son of God—sinless, holy and pure.

So isn't it striking that even in the middle of all this, Jesus still carved out quality time for his heavenly Father. He made time to ask for his help to be obedient. He prayed at the beginning of his ministry:

Very early in the morning, while it was still dark, Jesus got up, left the house and went off to a solitary place, where he prayed. Simon and his companions went to look for him, and when they found him, they exclaimed: "Everyone is looking for you!" (Mark 1 v 35-36)

And he prayed at the end of his ministry, on the night of his arrest:

> *He began to be deeply distressed and troubled ... he fell to the ground and prayed. (Mark 14 v 33, 35)*

If Jesus needed to pray, then you and I do too.

There's no better way to develop a new mind than to read the Bible as a child of God, sitting at the feet of our precious Father. It's not an academic text requiring textual analysis. It's the words of our Dad, who loves us. His stories are there to inspire us, not just inform us. His commands are there to mould us, not just intrigue us. His words are designed to help us love him and live for him, not just grasp doctrinal nuances. There's no better way to approach the God who wants to change us than as a child in need of her Father: humbly, tenderly, gently, honestly, excitedly, intimately.

What difference would it make to you to start a quiet time, every morning, with a simple prayer not just asking for God's help to understand the passage, but with a plea that the passage will help you appreciate Jesus' love, and grow in his likeness, a little more? What might change if you ended that time thinking about the day ahead and specifically thinking through how you can use the Scripture you have read to prepare you for the next few hours?

What difference would it make to you to go to a Bible-study group prepared to be honest about your struggles; willing to ask for your sisters' help to develop new, beautiful thoughts; and determined not to allow others to make excuses for your sin?

Your thoughts may seem out of control. Feral, almost. But

they don't need to be. It may take years, but they can be tamed. They can become pure.

New self

There's no way of keeping it in. No method of suppressing the new self. If we have really grasped our new identity, really begun to be renewed in our minds, then it will show in our lives. The change may be a trickle rather than a torrent, but it will be there and it will be there for others to see.

What will it look like? Like Jesus—like "true righteousness and holiness" (Ephesians 4 v 24). We will be people who joyfully do what God says is right, living in ways that are pure and distinct from the world around us.

And here again, there are ways in which we can be active in putting on our new clothes.

Have you ever counted how many hours a week you spend in fantasy land or surfing porn sites? Have you ever worked out how much money you have spent in a year on subscriptions, ungodly books, sex toys or provocative films? Have you ever estimated how many opportunities you have lost to show love or share the gospel with the people around you, because you allowed yourself to be drawn into day-dreams or more.

I did those sums once. It wasn't an encouraging figure.

Putting on our new self means letting the priorities that God has put in our heart start to ooze out of our being. It means becoming wise stewards of the time, money and relationships that God has entrusted to our care. Even if we have only been involved in fantasy and pornography on a small scale, it's amazing what opportunities can open up when we seek God's kingdom rather than pursuing our idols.

Instead of running to fantasy when real relationships get tough, we can choose to spend time investing in relationships—praying for the ability to forgive, disciplining ourselves to be generous to those who hurt us, deciding to write a card of encouragement to those who we find irritating, inviting out for coffee those who drain us, and serving those who don't think about how to serve us. That's what it means to be Christ-like.

Instead of losing ourselves in the comforting world of pornography, we can choose to remember God's comfort for us, and choose to pass that comfort on to others who suffer by supporting organisations who stop sex trafficking. That's what it means to be Christ-like.

Instead of spending money on things that are sexually immoral, we can choose to be generous to family, friends, church, mission organisations and social-action projects. That's what it means to be Christ-like.

And we can and will make all these choices if we remember who we are, and to whom we belong. We don't have to screw ourselves up into a knot and somehow find the strength to do this all by ourselves. We can love radically, forgive frequently, give generously, and listen attentively, because God has first done all those things for us and is changing us—and those around us—so we can do those things for others.

And remarkably, in all this giving, we will find ourselves being blessed. We will find ourselves enjoying a reality that is so much more satisfying than the self-centred fake world we had indulged in. We will find that purity is not only possible, but it is wonderful.

Ten steps to changing your clothes

It's a daily challenge. For the rest of our lives, we have the opportunity to consistently dump our dirty rags, and replace them with garments of beauty. So, if you haven't already, let's get started on the practicalities. Grab your pen or your tablet and put your own life under the microscope. There's no time like the present! Work your way through these questions—they're based on the chapters you've been reading—and start your journey to true beauty and purity.

1. What action(s) do I need to stop?
2. What idol(s) fuel this action and what aspect of God's character am I doubting?
3. What repentance needs to take place?
4. What truths about God do I need to remember? Which passages of Scripture teach these truths?
5. What practical steps can I take to battle temptation?
6. What aspects of my identity do I need to recall?
7. What godly character traits can I develop to replace my ungodly ones; what Bible passages will help me do this?
8. What can I be praying for myself today?
9. What positive steps can I take to act like Jesus right here and now?
10. What accountability would be good for me? Who can I call later to get that accountability started?

9. Intimacy

I am not always very good at perseverance.

Every now and then, I decide to take up something new. I throw myself into the venture with a passion and then a few months later, the idea fizzles out.

Partly fuelled by my love of *The Lord of the Rings*, I decided to learn to ride earlier this year. I bought the boots, I booked the lessons, I even read the wikihow pages on riding a horse. Thoroughly excited, I bounced to the stables. I was going to canter across the plains, wind in my hair, like in the films.

Alas, the reality of horse-riding is not so romantic. It's hard to get on and off a horse; trotting pounds the muscles in your legs like few other forms of exercise; and when men on mopeds drive up behind you and rev their engines, horses spin round at quite an alarming speed. Horse-riding can hurt and it can be scary!

So I stopped. I did want to learn to ride, but I only wanted to ride if it was easy. Once it got hard, I wanted to give up.

Thankfully, God doesn't mind if I don't keep learning to ride a horse. He does mind about my purity though, and my pursuit of it. He minds about yours, too.

So let me pose a couple of questions:

1. How much do you want this purity we've been exploring?
2. Are you still going to pursue it even when it gets tough?

It won't be easy

Because it will be tough. Memories of the past, circumstances in the present and stresses about the future can all encourage us to dump the progress towards purity we've made. And Satan doesn't want us to become more like Jesus—he will seek to work through the people around us, or our own wayward desires, and encourage us to return to the idols of control, relationships and experience, and all the ungodliness they bring.

Purity is not going to be easy. It will be tempting to give up. It will sometimes seem elusive. But despite everything around and within us that holds us back, God makes it possible.

I'm never quite sure if it's good to have favourite verses of the Bible (after all, every single word is from God and stunningly important), but there are a couple of verses that are particularly special to me because a wise minister once shared them with me when I was thinking about giving up on various aspects of my walk with the Lord.

> *His divine power has given us everything we need for a godly life through our knowledge of him who called us by his own glory and goodness. Through these he has given us his very great and precious promises, so that through them you may participate in the divine nature, having escaped the corruption in the world caused by evil desires. (2 Peter 1 v 3-4)*

God has not left me, or you, unequipped. He has given his precious, chosen children everything we need. Purity might seem like a tough standard to aspire to, but God has given us the power we need. "His divine power"—the power that was at work in the making of the world and the miracles of the Gospels—is at work in us, making a godly life possible.

His power is strong enough to make his promises to us—to rescue us, live in us and lead us home—true. And that means that we can "participate in the divine nature" instead of joining in with "the corruption in the world".

Participate in the divine nature. We can know God—Father, Son and Spirit. We can enjoy intimacy with him. We can enjoy becoming more and more like him.

Every time we run back into Jesus' arms for forgiveness, our relationship with him is strengthened. Every time we make a choice to live in the light of our forgiveness and shun the pull of our old self, we reflect our Lord a little more. Every time we choose contentment or trust or prayer or self-control, we become more aligned with the One who knows us and loves us the best.

You can become more and more like Jesus, as you grow closer and closer to him. You *can* dump your old ways of thinking and behaving—you *can* put on those garments of loveliness. Those idols you have held dear in the past *can* be destroyed. That addiction to porn or that tendency to flee to fantasy when life gets tough *can* be tossed aside. You *can* become increasingly content in the Lord and ever more trusting in his sovereign ways. Each day you *can* reflect more of Jesus' beauty.

This is not a false hope; it's the real offer of a life focused on our precious Saviour, with his power at work in you to achieve this. It's a reality you can see lived out in the lives of thousands of women across the globe. It's a path that leads to ever increasing intimacy with your Maker and with your fellow-believers. It's a life God has made possible.

It will happen

I'll be honest with you—I'm not completely pure yet. Anyone who knows me can tell you that. I don't use pornography anymore—I can tell you, from personal experience, that the lure of online sex can be conquered. I don't read erotica—such books have been dumped from my bookcases and my shopping trips. There is freedom from that snare too. And I now see fantasy-land for what it truly is—a cheap substitute that will only ever push me further away from God. But I'm still tempted to go there… and some days, the desire is strong. And I'm still tempted to try to exert control over life rather than acknowledge Jesus as the loving King he truly is. Sometimes I stumble and fall. Frequently, I need my sisters in Christ to encourage me by reminding me of how great God is, how much I need his mercy, and how certainly I have it.

But one day I will be completely pure. You will be too, if you are following Jesus. God promises, through the apostle John:

> *Dear friends, now we are children of God, and what we will be has not yet been made known. But we know that when Christ appears, we shall be like him, for we shall see him as he is. (1 John 3 v 2)*

When we see Jesus face to face, we shall be like him: fully pure in every aspect of our lives. At that moment, and for all eternity, there won't be a hint of sin or struggle left in our beings. No fantasies, no pornography, no lust, no adultery, no idols of any form. And we will be free to live in a perfect world where we will be completely fulfilled and in perfect relationship with our Saviour, and with those around us.

That's your future. God has made purity certain.

Until we get there, let's remember that our struggles won't last for ever. Let's remember we're forgiven when we fail, and that we have God's power working in us to change. Let's strive for, and enjoy, increasing purity, because we know where we're headed:

All who have this hope in him purify themselves, just as he is pure. (v 3)

It can be yours

There is a rumour going round that women don't watch online sex. There's a school of thought that says that our fantasies are romantic rather than explicit. Some argue that we don't think as visually as men, so pornography is rarely appealing. A few believe that we are, by nature, more pure and innocent.

I wish the rumours were right. They're not. Not in my experience, and not in the experience of most women I know.

But there's another rumour going round… that there is a way out. That, in Jesus, God offers forgiveness and change.

I'm so glad that rumour is true; that it can be the experience of any and every woman, including you.

Eternity is open.

Purity is possible.

Frequently asked questions

Is it OK to watch pornography with my husband?
Watching porn with your spouse certainly takes away the secrecy of the experience, but there are still some tough questions to be asked about why you would want to watch other people simulate pleasurable sex (sometimes under coerced conditions).

If you have problems in your sexual relationship, this can be very distressing, but there are more reputable books written by sex therapists where you can look for solutions to the problems you may be having. These will give you ideas or reassurance from people who understand marital struggles, and this is a far better strategy than trying to glean tips from actors and actresses in the adult industry.

If you want to use porn to spice up your love-life, then alarm bells need to be sounding in your mind. Watching another man (or woman) get aroused will not give long-term help to your own sex life—it is far more likely that you will find it increasingly difficult to get aroused without the help of porn, and your relationship may well suffer as a result. The Bible is clear that:

> *Marriage should be honoured by all, and the marriage bed kept pure, for God will judge the adulterer and all the sexually immoral. (Hebrews 13 v 4)*

Thinking lustfully about someone on screen is inner adultery. Porn is not a gateway to purity in marriage.

What should I do if I discover my teenage daughter watching pornography?

It can be a massive shock to walk in on your daughter and see her using pornography, or to look at your browser history and know beyond any reasonable doubt that your teen (or child) has been investigating those kinds of sites. The temptation is to panic, cry or react out of anger—but none of those things help.

Here are some tips on how to approach the situation:

1. Pray: you are going to need God's perspective, love and strength.
2. Fix a time to chat: somewhere quiet, maybe out of the house, certainly without other family members being in earshot.
3. Love: tell your daughter that you love her, and that will never change, and that God loves her too.
4. Listen: ask her to explain what she has been doing and to outline why. Did she simply open a link sent to her by a friend? (The culture of sexting—sending provocative photos or videos to peers—is rife, and it may be that she didn't intend to watch anything

specifically pornographic at all.) Has her porn use been a one-off, regular, or is it an addiction? Is she simply wondering what sex is like, or trying to keep up with what her friends know or are doing (or are claiming to be doing), or trying to find out how to do something to try with a boy (or girl) at school, or trying to compensate for loneliness? Try to work out which idol(s) is at play in her life. And check to see if she has been watching porn elsewhere—is there a particular friend who is encouraging porn use?

5. Explain: that porn is not what real sex is like—it's a poor teacher and a pointless substitute. Using it will damage current and future relationships. Show what the Bible says about God's love for us, his forgiveness, his call to purity and his Spirit's enabling to be faithful even when we are struggling.

6. Ask: what she would like to do next? See if she asks for help to stop. See if she offers an apology. Or see if she is more interested in excusing it, belittling it, or covering it up ("You won't tell anyone else, will you?")

7. Enforce boundaries: beef up the security setting with your ISP (internet service provider), set up Covenant Eyes (covenanteyes.com) and, most importantly, tell her that you will be asking her how she is getting on in avoiding porn; say that you will need to check her mobile phone regularly to help her pursue purity. Talk to other mothers if appropriate, so they can support their children.

8. Memorise Scripture: pick a verse and learn it together over the coming days.

9. Set aside regular time: to talk and pray about the underlying issues (her idol of experience or her feelings or loneliness and so on).

10. Pray: with her and for her.

Of course, if she has rejected Christianity, some of the above may fall on deaf ears, but it is good to give a biblical perspective anyway.

How do I remove pornography from my computer?

If you've been downloading porn for some time, there may well be a wealth of ungodly material sitting on your laptop just waiting to reel you back in. If you want to pursue true beauty in Jesus, the best course of action is to get rid of it as soon as you can.

1. Find each image and each video and hit delete. Or ask a friend to do it for you.

2. Go into your trash folder or recycle bin and delete them again—get them right away from your machine.

3. Go to your browser and hit "clear history" or "clear browsing data" and delete any pornography shortcuts that may be sitting on your navigation bar or in your bookmarks.

4. Cancel any subscriptions and remove yourself from any chat rooms, website accounts or email lists that promote sexually explicit material.

5. Up the security settings with your internet service provider (ISP) to something more family friendly. Get them to block porn sites to keep temptation at bay.

6. Finally, register with an organisation such as Covenant

Eyes (covenanteyes.com). The fee for the full service is worth it. It will make you accountable to wise, mature Christian friends for the way you use your computer.

Then do the same with any mobile devices that have been used for pornography too, and delete any adult channels from your TV. It will take a little time, but fleeing temptation is a great thing to do—it helps you become more like Jesus.

How do I start an accountability group in my church?

In any given church, it is likely that there is more than one woman using pornography. It can be a huge encouragement to meet together (probably no more than monthly) to spur one another on (Hebrews 10 v 24). But how on earth can you go about setting up something like this?

1. Chat to your minister. Any pastoral work ultimately comes under his authority and so asking for his wisdom is a good place to start. If it's easier, chat to your church's women's ministry co-ordinator first (if you have one). Both the pastor and women's worker may also have some good ideas on who the group would be suitable for.

2. Wait for a suitable sermon (if there is one coming up within the next couple of months). Linking the launch of the group to teaching on the subject makes it more likely that people will see their need.

3. Put up a poster saying where and when the group will meet (meeting in a church room is better than in a home). Ask the service leader to draw attention to the poster.

4. If you are brave enough, give your testimony in a service—how God has convicted you of your need for purity, how you are relying on his mercy, and how you are pursuing purity. It's nerve-wracking, but hugely encouraging.

5. Plan the first meeting:
   - Start the meeting with tea and coffee and some light-hearted conversation (everyone is bound to be nervous).
   - Pray.
   - Read a suitable Bible passage (Isaiah 61 is a particular favourite of mine) and draw out a few, relevant thoughts.
   - Set confidentiality parameters. It's best not to promise complete confidentiality—any criminal activity shared should be dealt with, and if anyone expresses self-destructive thoughts, help needs to be sought. Do promise that nothing that is said will be passed on without discussion with the individual first.
   - Give everyone a chance to share why they are there.
   - Set aims for the group (every group will be different, but the basic goals are usually to keep each other focused on Jesus and away from porn).
   - Agree format and frequency of future meetings (between once a month and once a term usually works). You could look at each idol in turn via a Bible study, have periods of sharing where people update on how they are doing, and end with a time of prayer.
   - Pray: in one big group or in pairs.
   - And then just keep meeting, and welcoming in new people as and when appropriate.

It's rare, but it is worth being aware that some people deeply entrenched in the bleakest aspects of pornography may use groups like this to try to recruit new, vulnerable people to their covert networks of bestiality or child abuse. It is worth making it clear that if any such attempts come to light, the person responsible will be reported to the proper authorities, though will also continue to be supported by other members of the church (outside the group).

Should I go to the police if I have been involved in child pornography?

It's worth saying that, if you are asking yourself this question, then God is clearly at work in your heart. Most people involved in criminal activity want to keep their actions covered—you are thinking of bringing them into the open, and that's a great sign of growth and change. Jesus' forgiveness covers all his followers, no matter what their crimes. But there is no suggestion in the Bible that the cross of Christ makes us immune from receiving the consequences of our actions in the here and now. Indeed, God's word says that government exists to punish crime and that we are to submit to that (Romans 13 v 1-7).

Accidentally downloading a single image of child pornography when you were looking for adult pornography is probably not something that warrants a criminal prosecution (simply get rid of the material as soon as you download it). But if you have been repeatedly or deliberately perpetuating child abuse by looking at the pictures taken by abusers— or if you have been circulating abusive pictures to others who enjoy child pornography—then you have broken the law, and confession to either the police or a mental-health professional (who can offer you residential treatment) is the right thing to do.

It may be one of the toughest decisions of your life. It will undoubtedly hurt those closest to you. But deeply entrenched sin sometimes needs radical action. Wholeness for you and hope for the abused children are worth the trauma of a police investigation and trial, desperately difficult though those things are.

Does God love Christians who are porn-users?

Yes. It's as simple as that. He loves you so much that he sent his Son to die for you, he sent his Spirit to live in you, and he loves you so much that he wants you to change…

Thank you...

... to all the godly and patient people who have loved, gently rebuked, prayed for and inspired me as I have struggled to learn what it means to pursue purity.

... to the many women who have shared with me their battles with fantasy and pornography—it has been such a privilege to know you, point you to your loving Lord, and see you change.

... to those specific people who have allowed their stories to be shared in the pages of this book—praise God for his work in you!

... to my lovely prayer partners, Hilary Nicholls and Alison Miller, and to Dorothy Mallett, whose support and sanity have helped me persevere through every page of writing.

... to Andrew Nicholls and the wonderful team at Dundonald Church, Raynes Park, London, whose faithful teaching and wise pastoring help me to look to Jesus each and every day.

... to Carl Laferton, editor extraordinaire, whose prayerful wisdom and wit has made the writing and publishing process such an absolute delight.

... to all those who have read this book. The whole writing thing really doesn't work without you.

thegoodbook

COMPANY

BIBLICAL | RELEVANT | ACCESSIBLE

At The Good Book Company, we are dedicated to helping Christians and local churches grow. We believe that God's growth process always starts with hearing clearly what he has said to us through his timeless word—the Bible.

Ever since we opened our doors in 1991, we have been striving to produce Bible-based resources that bring glory to God. We have grown to become an international provider of user-friendly resources to the Christian community, with believers of all backgrounds and denominations using our books, Bible studies, devotionals, evangelistic resources, and DVD-based courses.

We want to equip ordinary Christians to live for Christ day by day, and churches to grow in their knowledge of God, their love for one another, and the effectiveness of their outreach.

Call us for a discussion of your needs or visit one of our local websites for more information on the resources and services we provide.

Your friends at The Good Book Company

thegoodbook.com | thegoodbook.co.uk
thegoodbook.com.au | thegoodbook.co.nz
thegoodbook.co.in